Lee Tilghman

Simon & Schuster

New York   Amsterdam/Antwerp   London   Toronto   Sydney/Melbourne   New Delhi

If You Don't Like This, I Will Die

AN INFLUENCER MEMOIR

Simon & Schuster
1230 Avenue of the Americas
New York, NY 10020

For more than 100 years, Simon & Schuster has championed authors and the stories they create. By respecting the copyright of an author's intellectual property, you enable Simon & Schuster and the author to continue publishing exceptional books for years to come. We thank you for supporting the author's copyright by purchasing an authorized edition of this book.

No amount of this book may be reproduced or stored in any format, nor may it be uploaded to any website, database, language-learning model, or other repository, retrieval, or artificial intelligence system without express permission. All rights reserved. Inquiries may be directed to Simon & Schuster, 1230 Avenue of the Americas, New York, NY 10020 or permissions@simonandschuster.com.

Copyright © 2025 by Lee Tilghman

All rights reserved, including the right to reproduce this book or portions thereof in any form whatsoever. For information, address Simon & Schuster Subsidiary Rights Department, 1230 Avenue of the Americas, New York, NY 10020.

Many names and some identifying details have been changed.

First Simon & Schuster hardcover edition August 2025

SIMON & SCHUSTER and colophon are registered trademarks of Simon & Schuster, LLC

Simon & Schuster strongly believes in freedom of expression and stands against censorship in all its forms. For more information, visit BooksBelong.com.

For information about special discounts for bulk purchases, please contact Simon & Schuster Special Sales at 1-866-506-1949 or business@simonandschuster.com.

The Simon & Schuster Speakers Bureau can bring authors to your live event. For more information or to book an event, contact the Simon & Schuster Speakers Bureau at 1-866-248-3049 or visit our website at www.simonspeakers.com.

Interior design by Ruth Lee-Mui

Manufactured in the United States of America

1 3 5 7 9 10 8 6 4 2

Library of Congress Cataloging-in-Publication Data has been applied for.

ISBN 978-1-6680-5150-4
ISBN 978-1-6680-5152-8 (ebook)

*To whichever bloodline/DNA strand
gave me the bold ability to
speak up and share my story*

If You Don't Like This, I Will Die

Prologue

"Wait, aren't you Lee From America?"

I was with Jordan, Adelaide, and Mackenzie, waiting in line at Hugo's Tacos as we always did on Monday nights—the sapphire twilight descending across East Los Angeles. I paused when I heard the voice from behind us. The sound of a chipper, young, energetic thing.

It was a follower.

This was confirmed once I turned to look at her.

Perfect golden tan. No-makeup makeup. Tiny gold hoop earrings. Leggings that made her thighs look too good. A neutral-colored hooded cropped sweatshirt with CorePower Yoga's logo across her chest. The poppy-rounded choker I'd promoted with a special code, LEE10, which was redeemed six thousand times, causing it to sell out overnight. She looked like most of my followers. Which is to say, she looked like me a few months ago, before I left that all behind.

I had short hair now, a bowl cut, and I was rounder now, softer. I was wearing expressive makeup, glitter on my eyelids and yellow eyeliner on my lash line. I wasn't so orange now either, as I wasn't eating fifteen big carrots from the Hollywood Farmers' Market every day to keep my blood sugar low. Eating carrots was one of the hundred conscious and subconscious behaviors I did throughout the day to avoid sugar, my greatest fear. I wasn't as bony now. I had fuller cheeks and the glint back in my eyes. You could no longer see all the veins in my neck. My jawbone didn't jut out like it used to.

This physical transformation had so far kept me from being recognized by my nearly four hundred thousand Instagram followers. For months, I had successfully kept my former life as an influencer from my treatment friends. When they asked me what I did, I didn't lie, I just skillfully dodged the question. They worked as teachers, therapists, and dog trainers. They didn't like me for my online fame. Their friendship had provided a cocoon, a pillowy calm amid a shift away from such a massive part of my life. I didn't want that old life encroaching on this new one. And certainly not here at Hugo's, where we came every week to eat tacos, drink horchata, smoke cigarettes, gossip, and laugh. Hugo's was my safe haven, away from the sceney LA influencer life.

Not anymore.

"You're Lee, right?" the girl asked.

I cleared my throat and noticeably switched from the loud, goofy Lee I had just been thirty seconds prior to a quieter, more timid self.

"Hi," I said.

"I've been a fan for so long." She let out a nervous laugh. "My sister and I loved all your stuff. We always sent—"

"Thank you," I said, interrupting her. I smiled with my eyes and turned back around to my friends. Immediately, I was flooded with the feeling I'd get whenever I'd post something on Instagram. How if just one person doesn't like me, it's all over for me. How my job is to be liked, adored, admired, and envied. How being an influencer had, within a few short years, rocketed me to this weird level of fame, and now when I was doing errands and living in the IRL world, they could affect the URL world too.

I was surprised by how quickly the feelings came rushing back, how familiar and awful they felt. Would this girl think I was a bitch for mostly ignoring her? Would she go on some influencer-snark subreddit and write about how I wasn't nice enough? A fellow influencer had told me there was a thread about me on the blogsnark subreddit (196,000 members and counting). All the big influencers had one. These were dark corners of the web where people who hate-followed you could band together in their general disgust and aversion toward you. Every move you made, story you posted, or person from your past could be posted on that thread, and overnight they could stage a smear campaign and you could be canceled—like I had been.

The family ahead of us finished paying and moved aside. We made a few automatic steps toward the ordering window.

"So, what are you guys going to get?" I said, doing my best to recapture the carefree fun we'd been having before the girl in the leggings showed up.

"Wait, what was she talking about?" Jordan asked.

"Are you famous?" Mackenzie asked, exhaling a giant puff of strawberry vape.

The blood rushed to my face, a million little prickles where every freckle was.

"Yeah," Adelaide said, "who's Lee From America?"

It was a good question—one I'd only recently been trying to figure out myself. The short answer was that Lee From America had been a successful blogger and then an even more successful influencer, one of the very first to make a career of it in the Instagram wellness space, earning nearly $300,000 a year for posting vibrant pictures of farmer's market salads, overflowing smoothies, and contorted yoga poses. Lee From America was a girl with pearly white teeth and a perfectly styled "messy" bun (that of course she made a video tutorial of) and skin unblemished from regular blue seaweed algae masks. Lee From America was me.

But it was more complicated than that. Because Lee From America wasn't me at all, and I really didn't know who I was because everything I once owned—my furniture, my clothes, even right down to the Elfa organization system inside my closet—had been gifted to me by brands to post on social media. The realization that both my inner and outer worlds were entangled in corporate sponsorships, likes, tags, discount codes, Q&As, and referrals led to crippling anxiety, mounting paranoia, and, ultimately, a return to the disordered eating I had struggled with years earlier.

Things had gotten so bad, I don't know if I'd be here if I hadn't gotten help.

I didn't want to be Lee From America anymore. I'd been spending the last few months deprogramming myself from that person—the girl who chased thinness, radiance, and perfection, stumbled into internet spaces that reinforced those ideals, then let them consume her until she couldn't separate her identity from her gluten-free diet.

Once my friends knew, would they desert me? Either because of who I'd been or because I withheld it from them—or both?

I had no choice now. I couldn't keep it from them any longer. Once we got our food and sat down at our usual bench, I would tell them everything, starting from the very beginning.

One

My life online officially started the day I was twelve and my father brought home a large box from Best Buy. He lugged it up from his sedan's trunk and placed it on a table in the living room. My mother, older sister, Lexie, and I all stood around as he got out his box cutter.

"We definitely don't want to scratch this!" he said.

This was our family's first computer. The only other one I'd seen inside someone's home belonged to my friend Natalie. Natalie's family had just moved from New York City to Connecticut after 9/11. She brought along with her a sophisticated level of consumerism I'd never seen before. Along with her Paul Frank pajamas, NARS makeup, and an HBO subscription so we could watch *Sex and the City*, she had an iMac in her room. It was part transparent plastic, part blue, and all fashionable. After school, we'd go up to her room and log on to something called AIM where you could write instant messages back and forth to friends. It was better than passing notes in school. You didn't have to worry about a teacher intercepting them and giving you detention.

The monitor my dad lifted out of the box and placed on the table was not a Mac. It was a Dell. I didn't care. I gasped and reached out to rip off the plastic film screen protector.

"Not yet, Lee—hold on."

I hovered over my dad, breathing down his neck as he rummaged through the boxes.

"What else do you need to do? Isn't this it?"

It was that day that I learned the screen was just a screen. Back then, the actual computer was a whole other component: a large metal box that was so big it needed to be under the table.

He brought several other boxes from the car and proceeded to open and unpack them. There was the computer, two speakers, a router, a modem, and a printer.

I was antsy. My father, impatient with my impatience, shooed me away. These were expensive items, and my wild hands might break them.

"I'll let you know when it's out of the box."

I went into the family room to watch cartoons, keeping an eye on the door to the living room, waiting to be summoned.

"Lee? Lex?" my dad finally called.

My mother, sister, and I all stood around Dad as he booted up the computer. He put his hands on his hips, looking proud as the Windows logo danced across the screen.

He'd given our family of four access to the World Wide Web in our very own home.

We jumped around, clapping, hugging, and smiling.

One at a time, we sat at the "computer chair"—just an unused dining room chair at this point—and took turns playing around with it. When it was my turn, I reveled in the clickity-clack-clack sound of the keyboard, punching letters and testing out the different fonts in Microsoft Word, which came on a separate CD-ROM my father had bought alongside everything else. We'd been taking typing lessons at school so we could learn to type without looking down. My father watched and noted how quickly I typed. Everyone always noted how quickly—and loudly—I typed. I've never been graceful.

Within a few hours, unable to calm down from the excitement, I begged my parents to download AIM. I chose the username glitterbug46. Then I immediately signed on and added my friends to my "Buddies" list by typing in their screen names (which I'd already memorized by heart). I felt the overwhelming sense of possibility that AIM provided me: an opportunity to differentiate myself and to understand who I was outside the confines of my conservative town. Then, my mother barged into the living room.

"That's enough computer time for today, Lee."

My mom introduced a thirty-minutes-per-day rule for the computer. Over the next few weeks, I used my daily half hour to build out my AIM profile:

> BFFAEA: Skidoo, Milly, Katy, Maggie, Natalie!!!!!
>
> He doesn't even know you're there, no no
>
> He don't love your eyes
>
> He don't love your smile
>
> —Girlfriend, N*Sync
>
> HOEZ B4 BROZ!

A few weeks later, I got a boyfriend named Toby. He was a shy, sweet boy in my seventh-grade class. All our friends were dating each other, and since we were the only single people left in the group, they matched us up together. We'd never spoken in person before. I had never even been within five feet of him.

Naturally, we got to know each other on AIM. He used a

cobalt-blue Comic Sans font. Within days, he told me he loved me, and I told him I loved him too. I changed my AIM profile to:

Taken by Toby

Love u 4ever babe

Each day after school, I'd rush home to chat with Toby online. I loved how safe talking on the internet felt—and how naturally it came to me.

Our romance finally went IRL at Neon Nights, a monthly dance at our local YMCA, where the rec room was transformed into a party room with flashing lights, streamers, and a DJ. Chaperones hovered around the perimeter, enforcing the arm's-length rule that prohibited grinding or wandering hands.

Our friend group organized for us to have a big kiss that night. Toby's friends told him to meet me on the dance floor at seven thirty, and my friends told me to do the same. I was terribly embarrassed and had no desire to kiss Toby, but I succumbed to peer pressure. At exactly seven thirty, our friends created a big circle around us. They began chanting "Kiss, kiss, kiss!" and some other kids joined in on the heckling. We had to do it quickly before the chaperones broke it up.

For the first time ever, I got a good look at Toby. He was wearing cargo shorts with fifteen pockets. His black greasy hair was cut in a mushroom style. He had a few pimples. He smiled slyly to reveal his braces. I had braces too.

I wasn't attracted to Toby. I really didn't want to kiss him. He kept weird, long eye contact with me as we stood across from each other in the big circle. Toby shrugged, as if to say, "Let's do this!" The next thing I knew, we were pushed together by our friends, and our mouths smashed, braces clanking, noses unsure where to go. The thin skin on the inside of my lip broke as my braces dug in, and I tasted blood. Our friends cheered. The chaperones separated us. It was horrible, but my first kiss was over with.

Six weeks later, Toby and I broke up, and I spent more time on the computer, which had been moved from the living room to the sunroom. On weekend mornings, my sister and I rotated between games like *The Sims*, *Age of Empires*, and *RollerCoaster Tycoon*. She taught me *Sims* cheat codes, and I took mental notes on where she'd place her roller coasters. I loved watching her play games. It was the second-best thing to playing the games myself.

I developed a new weekday routine where I'd come home from tennis practice, grab a bowl of pretzels, run through the swinging kitchen door into the sunroom, and log on to AIM to talk to my friends. Even though we saw each other all day—on our walks to and from school, at lunch, and sometimes even at after-school sports—we all started to live more of our lives online. Nobody ever wanted to log off. And so the away message became a status symbol: The longer you kept it on, the cooler you were.

BRB, getting a snack

Hanging with my homies

Dinner time!

Doing H/W . . . BBL [be back later]

One of my friends even kept her away message on for an entire week while she was on vacation! My mom would never let me do that. Even as I entered high school and gained more autonomy, she made us turn off the computer every night to save electricity. I loved playing around with the different AIM fonts. With each new typeface and color combination, I dreamed of an alternative Lee. A Lee who wasn't a self-conscious, braces-wearing, loud-typing girl. A Lee who was confident, who could have conversations with friends that were too hard to have in person, who thought nothing of chatting with cute guys that she would never go up to in real life.

Like Adrian.

He was a sophomore—a grade higher than me. Adrian skateboarded, wore all black, and drove a beat-up car. He was different from the Vineyard Vines–wearing boys I'd hung around with in junior high. He also had a girlfriend he'd been with for a few years. A cheerleader. He and I had never spoken at school, but one night he sent me a chat request on AIM. We chatted every day after school yet continued not to share more than a glance in the school hallways. When word got out that we were chatting on AIM, some of the cheerleading squad began posting away messages about me, calling me a slut. One also said it to my face at school: "Watch your step, slut, or you're gonna get it." The threats overwhelmed me. Adrian didn't try to comfort me, and he didn't face the same harassment. He just stopped messaging me.

It quickly became clear just how much sex and desire were bound up with the internet. My friends and I started experimenting with chat rooms, pretending we were much older and giggling at the weirdos who asked for sex. I even met a boy outside of my school on Facebook. At the time, Facebook was only for college students, but my sister got me a digital invite and I was able to have a Facebook page at fourteen, two years before it was opened to the public. This boy, who also somehow finagled an account, lived a few towns over from me. My parents let him come over for pizza and a movie, on the condition they hung out with us too. I was absolutely not allowed to be in the house alone with a boy.

I broke this rule one afternoon shortly before the end of freshman year. Sitting on AIM, eating my usual bowl of pretzels and procrastinating studying for my biology final, I got a message.

Hey. Wut r u doing?

It was Landon. He was a junior and one of the most popular boys in school. He was an incredible athlete, drove a Range Rover, and had a year-round tan and curly brown hair that made his electric-blue eyes that much more striking. Rumor had it that he was interested in both me and a classmate and was in the final stages of deciding who would be his next hookup now that he was single again.

"She's got the big boobs, but you've got the face," my friend said, assuring me.

The heavens aligned and Landon somehow chose me. I'd never felt particularly attractive or desired before in my life. I knew then and there that my life would never be the same. The most popular guy in school wanted *me*. The junior girls he hung out with were so cool and mature. They wore Juicy Couture terry cloth skirts, Lacoste polos, Jack Rogers sandals, and Lancôme Juicy Tubes on their lips. Their hair was so straightened it looked scorched, the flyaways sticking up like fried antennas.

At the sight of his message, I inhaled sharply, my heart racing. I told myself to seem cool, but I had no idea how to do that.

Nm, studying for biology. U?

Need help studying? I've taken that class b4.
I can help you. I'm older, remember? haha

My mother and sister had taken a skiing trip to Utah that week, and my dad was at his office a few towns away. He usually didn't get home until around six o'clock. That gave us about two hours of freedom.

Sure. Come over!

I ran upstairs to get ready, squealing with excitement. Nikki, our yellow Lab, followed me to see what all the fuss was about. I stripped off my Soffe shorts and put on my favorite Abercrombie low-rise jeans. For a top, I chose a reversible Abercrombie shirt, with one side reading I LOVE YOU and the other I LOVE YOU NOT. I chose the I LOVE YOU side. I went back downstairs and spread my biology binder across the living room coffee table. I really did need to study. I wanted to get a good grade. My parents were concerned about my grades in math and science.

Suddenly, I heard Landon knocking on the back door. I let him in. Nikki greeted him too. Landon followed me the few short steps from the mudroom into the family room. His blue eyes shone beneath his big bushy eyebrows. He sat down on the couch next to me, not bothering to acknowledge the open binder.

"It's so cool to see your house," he said.

I nodded and let out a little giggle.

Suddenly, Landon leaned in, squeezed the back of my neck, and went for my face. I moved my mouth up and down, trying to get a rhythm with his tongue, which never quite happened. He started unbuttoning my pants, reaching his fingers along the hem of my underwear, pushing them inside. He shoved two fingers inside of me. This was all happening so fast I could barely grasp it. It was so weird to make out with someone while the sun was still shining. The few times I'd made out with boys, it was always in the dark.

Landon suddenly pulled away, his eyes half closed, sedated with horniness. "Lee," he said, "do you know how to give a blow job?"

I knew the term. I'd heard that some girls practiced on bananas and carrots. We talked about it at sleepovers.

"I don't . . ." I sputtered, looking away. "I don't know. I've never done that."

Landon laughed. "Aw, that's okay. I can teach you."

He unzipped his pants and lifted his hips off the couch, belt clanging on the floor.

"Get on your knees," he instructed.

I got on my knees.

With a smirk across his face, he held his erection inches from me, swirling his cock between his fingers. It waved in front of me like a flag.

"You're just going to put it in your mouth," he said, guiding the tip of his cock into my mouth. As soon as it was between my lips, he lifted his hips, causing his penis to enter the length of my mouth. I gagged.

"Oops." He laughed. "Sorry! Just . . . yeah. Keep your teeth away."

I focused on the task at hand. I bobbed my head up and down, encasing his penis in my mouth, keeping my teeth away and giving as much lip and tongue as I could. Landon moaned, first intermittently, then deeper, longer, and more intense. His breathing became sharp. He kept both hands on my head. My jaw began to lock up, but I pushed through.

Landon's hips began to move more erratically. He inhaled, exhaled. I didn't stop.

Suddenly, I heard the familiar sound of feet coming up the wooden back steps. Just as the back door opened, a warm, sour, chlorine-like substance filled my mouth. I pulled my mouth off of Landon's cock just in time to look up and see my dad, staring at his fifteen-year-old daughter on her knees in front of the couch my mother had just reupholstered in yellow-and-pink farmhouse checker.

Landon quickly got to his feet, pulling up his pants. I swallowed the substance and stood up, fumbling the button of my jeans. I didn't want my dad to see my underwear showing.

My father's mouth was agape, his eyes wide, his face frozen in shock.

"Lee," he said, almost too calmly, staring at the ground near my feet. "Go upstairs. Now."

He pointed toward the stairs.

"But, Dad—"

"Now!" he shouted.

I ran upstairs. I didn't know what was about to happen to Landon, and I didn't care. I was just thankful to be out of that space. I went into the bathroom, turned on the faucet, and washed my mouth out, gargling. A few minutes passed. I heard their voices talking. Then the back door shut. I ran into my bedroom and looked out the window to watch Landon's Rover driving away.

I heard my father come up the stairs, his pacing of the steps slow and deliberate. Tears welled in my eyes. I was so humiliated. My dad came in. On his face was a look of fury and anger so deep that I thought, *My father hates me.* He looked down at the carpet. He couldn't even look me in the eyes, and wouldn't be able to for an entire year.

"You're grounded," he said. "I'm not sure what your punishment is yet. I'm going to wait until your mother gets home to discuss what your punishment will be. I plan to call Landon's parents."

"Dad!" I wailed.

"You were supposed to be studying. Your grades have been lacking. And instead you're having guys over? You know that's against our rules!"

"Dad, please—"

"He's lucky I didn't knock him between the eyes. In my house. Who does he think he is?"

"But Dad, it's not his—"

"My daughter, a slut."

He walked out of my room, went to his bedroom, and slammed the door.

I needed comfort. So I did what was now feeling natural and instinctive. I turned to the internet. I ran downstairs to go on AIM.

I furiously typed to my friends.

> OMG U GUYS!!! I gave Landon a
> BJ and my dad walked in!!!

WHAT?!!!!!

Landon saw that I was online and messaged me.

Lee. I'm all good but that was crazy haha. U shouldn't have put the sink on upstairs, we could hear it. It was obvious wut u were trying 2 get out of ur mouth.

> Omg, landon, i'm so sorry.

The next day at school, it was all anyone could talk about. Some people whispered when I walked by, but most people didn't even try to conceal it. There was even a rumor going around that my dad had threatened Landon with a golf club, chasing him down the driveway with a 9-iron.

My mom had returned from her ski trip and was waiting for me when I got home from school.

"I heard what happened," she said. "And I read about it too—on your AIM."

It was the first time I wished I'd signed out. Dad hadn't turned the computer off overnight. My mom had read through the messages I'd sent to my friends.

"You're grounded for two weeks," she said. "No going out, no seeing friends."

She saved the worst punishment for last.

"And no computer."

Two

The dynamic with my sister had shifted a few years before, when she entered high school. She started going to the gym and reading *Cosmopolitan*. Games on the computer turned into private conversations with her friends on AIM. Instead of letting me watch her computer time like I used to from a seat scooched behind her, now she'd tell me to leave the room.

"You're annoying me! Get out!"

I'd go stiff, clutching my plastic Tupperware of Snyder's pretzels close to my chest, holding my ground.

"Mom!" she'd shout. "Lee's bothering me!"

Soon my mother would open the French doors and I'd be forced out. My sister was building her own sense of identity as she entered adolescence, and I felt left behind.

By the time she was a senior, my sister became a foreign, untouchable object in our house. As her studies ramped up and she prepared for college admissions and SATs, we were told to stay quiet in areas like the common room and the kitchen, where she liked to study. I saw how my parents shifted their lives around Lexie, and I was expected to as well.

I began coveting what Lexie had, envious of her place in the house. Lexie and I both got equal allowances and held summer jobs, but I tended to spend my money faster while Lexie accumulated her cash and spent more intentionally. I loved stealing her collared shirts from her closet. After wearing them, I'd put them back where I found them, only for Lexie to yell at me. She said she could tell I'd stolen them because of my deodorant residue and how the shirts were stretched. I just wanted to borrow Lexie's clothes like every other girl I knew did with her sister.

One evening as I was getting ready for a night out with friends, I snuck into her room and took her Longchamp Le Pliage handbag. I walked out the front door and yelled goodbye before my parents could see me with it.

I came home that night tipsy and dizzy and found my mother waiting for me in the family room. Her mouth was pursed, her voice stern. She walked up to me and tried to grab the bag from my hands while berating me for stealing. I held on to it, yelling at her to get away from me. We pulled each other's hair. I kicked and pulled away. We twisted under each other's slaps. I cried. She yelled. I didn't let go of the bag. To let go was to admit fault. My mother dug her nails into my skin. I dug my nails into her skin. I writhed myself out of her grip, finally letting her take the bag.

Up in my room, I peeled my mother's skin out from under my nails—the collection gruesome and putrid.

Our growing antagonism came to a head on Lexie's sixteenth birthday. Each year on our birthdays, we got to pick any dish for my dad to cook. He was incredibly gifted in the kitchen. That year, Lexie picked lobster. The preparations began in the early afternoon. We shucked corn and went to Stew Leonard's to pick out our lobsters. When we got home, my dad boiled the water and put the lobsters into the pot, telling us to leave the room while they screamed.

I showered and air-dried my hair in the late-summer heat,

putting on a tank top and shorts to stay cool. I headed downstairs. My parents were never big gift-givers, but I could see this birthday was going to be different. There was a tower of wrapped presents on the kitchen island.

During dinner, my parents handed her gift after gift. With each present Lexie unwrapped, my jealousy grew stronger. I couldn't believe what she was getting—the caliber of gifts was unmatched. Brand-new things from Vineyard Vines, the kind of stuff I only dreamed about. And for her last one, she unwrapped a little blue box from Tiffany's. It was from her godmother. She opened the box to find a Tiffany's key chain.

"I think there's something else, under that felt there," my mom said.

Lexie removed the felt from the box and showed us a set of keys to my grandmother's fifteen-year-old Volvo.

I seethed with envy, barely able to look at her.

I slammed my tiny lobster fork onto my plate, splattering butter and lobster juices across the wooden table.

"Lee!" my mother shouted, handing me a paper napkin. "Watch your manners and wipe up that oil stain before the wood absorbs it." She was always so worried about the furniture.

"No," I said. My anger overtook me and I felt myself slipping out of my body. I watched as I threw my paper napkin onto the floor.

I'd really started it now.

"This isn't fair. I can't believe Lexie gets all this stuff," I whined.

"That's just how it is!" my dad shouted at me. "When you turn sixteen, you'll get gifts too!"

Lexie and I had different godmothers. How could I be sure I'd also get the same Tiffany key chain on my sixteenth? And even though I'd probably eventually get the same Volvo when she left for college, it would still be *hers* first. I was always second in line.

I began crying, but I felt embarrassed. I knew I was getting too old for these sorts of tantrums. I tried to leave the room to go upstairs and process my feelings alone, but my father blocked the doorway like a starfish. I tried to wriggle past, my crying growing heavier as I wrestled against him. He used his legs and arms to keep me in the kitchen. "Let me go!" I cried. Tears fell down my face as I pleaded with him to let me exit.

"You've ruined my birthday dinner!" Lexie cried out.

"How could you make such a scene on your sister's special day?" my mom shouted. She was hysterical. I could tell the whole family was tired of my antics.

The more they yelled, the more I tried to get away. My sobbing turned jagged.

"Please let me go, please let me go!"

My father and I struggled. My mom moved in, and I kicked her—my signature move. She screamed at me. I felt ganged up on, three against one.

Finally, I wrestled free from my parents' grip. I looked down to see white fingerprints around my upper arm.

I stood in the doorway, staring at my family. I'd never felt more separate or less wanted in my life. Past them, on the table, I saw remnants of what could have been, what was supposed to be a peaceful, joyful night. Lobster forks. Melted butter. Wrapping paper. A beautiful summer's evening through the open French doors.

I wiped the snot from my face.

"I'm calling the cops!" I cried.

"DON'T YOU DARE CALL THE POLICE, LEE!" my mom yelled.

I ran upstairs to my bedroom, taking the stairs two at a time. I'd recently talked my parents into allowing me a telephone in my bedroom, after years of begging. With my heart pounding, I lay across my bed and reached for the Conair phone. I pressed the black squishy numbers and dialed 911. I wasn't sure what I wanted: Justice? To be saved? The act of pressing those little numbers felt both terrifying and thrilling. I'd threatened the call before, but this was the first time I was actually following through.

"Nine-one-one, what's your emergency?"

I froze and hung up. Moments later, the phones all around the house rang once, twice. I could hear my mother answer in a calm demeanor from the hallway downstairs. Moments later, she rapped on my door. Her voice penetrated through the wood.

"Lee, it's the police. They want to speak to you."

I put a pillow over my head.

"NO!" I screamed.

The muffled dark offered a contrived sense of safety. If only I could just stay here, everything would be all right.

I heard my mother open my door, the floor creaking. She touched the receiver to my arm.

"Lee, they need to speak to you. They know you called. They need to know everything is all right. Tell them everything is all right."

What had I done? Now that I'd involved the police, my parents weren't so bad anymore. But I didn't want to cave.

"NO!" I screamed again.

"Lee, I'm going to ask you one more time: Talk to them *now*." I felt the urgent anger underneath my mother's calm cloak.

I stayed still and said nothing.

"I'm so sorry, but she won't come to the phone. Everything's all right, but she won't come to the phone. She's just upset."

A pause.

"Okay, thank you."

She clicked off the cordless.

I opened the pillow an inch or two to check in with my mother's face.

"Well, look what you've done. The police are coming."

I got up, the pillow falling to the floor.

"They're what?" I asked.

"You wouldn't come to the phone to tell them everything's all right, so they need to come here and see—to make sure that everything really is all right."

As my mother left the room, I could hear my sister's cries from downstairs, echoing through the halls. "Are you kidding?" she wailed. "The cops are coming?"

We lived a few blocks away from the police station. Several minutes went by, then there was a booming knock on the front door.

"Hello, officers," my mother said in her friendliest voice. She often put on that bright, happy-go-lucky facade for others—even when things inside the house were far from it.

"Lee, get down here," my dad called up to me.

I got up, my body feeling fuzzy after lying down and crying for so long. I walked down the carpet-covered stairs to the foyer where everyone awaited me. Step by step, the policemen in their navy uniforms came into my view. One was tall, one was short. Both were wide and had buzz cuts.

I didn't have a bra on, and my cotton Gap spaghetti-strap tank top made me feel naked. My mother and sister had recently used the term "budding" when talking about my breasts. I could feel the cops' eyes on me, so I instinctively crossed my arms to cover my chest. Suddenly, I didn't want to be the center of attention anymore.

"Good evening, Lee," the taller one said. The shorter one held a notepad and clicked his pen. I paused on the stairs. There wasn't enough room for me in the foyer.

"Yeah, hi," I said.

"How are you doing this evening?" the taller one asked.

"Fine, thanks." The words hung in the air.

"Just got into a little fight with Mommy and Daddy?"

I looked at my sister, her eyes puffy and wet. She looked back at me with a sadness that overwhelmed me.

"Yeah," I said.

"It's my other daughter's sixteenth birthday tonight," my mom started, "and I think—"

"Just one second, ma'am." The tall one held up a hand in my mother's direction without breaking eye contact with me. "Can you uncover your arms for us, little lady?"

"Can I what?" I asked.

"Show us your arms," the shorter one said.

They wanted me to show that I didn't have any bruises or scratches. Would they notice my parents' fingerprints on my arms from earlier? What if Mom and Dad actually ended up getting arrested? I was even more terrified than when I'd placed the call, and this time there was no accompanying thrill. My stunt could potentially destroy my parents' lives. I waited a couple seconds longer, hoping that might be enough to fully erase any remnants of the fingerprints. But I knew the longer I delayed, the more suspicion I might rouse. I presented my arms to the officers.

"Thank you, little lady," the taller one said. The shorter one shut his notebook. They said goodbye and left.

My mother looked out the window as the policemen drove away. But I knew she wasn't watching them. She was looking to see if any of the neighbors were peering out of their own windows or had come out on their front stoops to see what was wrong at the Tilghmans'. She was always so concerned about what people thought of us. That was how it was for most of the families I grew up with in Connecticut—obsessed with maintaining an image of perfection. I despised this. As I lay in bed that night, I was delighted by the thought someone might have seen the police at our house.

And yet years later, I would behave the exact same way: posting photos on Instagram of my life, pretending it was perfect. At the time it wouldn't occur to me what a hypocrite I was being. All I would be thinking about was how to get more likes for my posts.

Three

My second year of high school, I developed a severe eating disorder. It began with a contest among my field hockey friends to see who could lose five pounds the fastest. One by one the other girls dropped out, calling the contest stupid and saying they loved food too much. But I kept going. On Sunday afternoons, my friends would upload pictures of the weekend's parties on Facebook. It was my favorite part of the week. I studied my body, the way my shoulder bones began to protrude, my arms shrinking and becoming straight lines. I loved the way this looked. My natural state, the Lee who was going through puberty and gaining weight, wasn't who I wanted to be, so I continued to alter my body through calorie restriction.

Five months after the contest began, as I was driving to school one morning, my body unconsciously steered the car into the parking lot of a CVS. I had no control over my actions. Possessed by starvation, I entered the store, marched to the candy aisle, and picked up a ten-ounce bag of peanut M&M's.

The moment I got outside, I ripped open the giant yellow bag and began shoveling the candies into my mouth, the months of deprivation coming undone. I got into the car and drove toward school, ramming handful after handful past my lips, barely chewing.

At a red light, I stowed the bag in the glove compartment so they'd be out of reach.

How could you do this? I thought. *How could you ruin your perfectly angular and delicate body?*

As soon as the light turned green, I steered with one knee and reached back into the glove compartment. I inhaled more M&M's. One or two dropped on the dirty floor. I picked them up and ate those too. After months of red bell peppers, hundred-calorie Special K snack bars, mini Dixie cups of Fiber One, and salad with no dressing, the fat and sugar of the candy was orgasmic. I had a boyfriend and we'd been having sex, and I even knew how to bring my body to orgasm. But nothing compared to the salty, chewy crunch of peanut M&M's. The sugar coursed through my bloodstream, and I practically shuddered from the sensation.

As soon as I caught sight of my school through the windshield, I felt another pang of guilt and disgust. Once in the school parking lot, I looked at my car's clock. Only three minutes until first bell. I looked into the near-empty bag.

"Aw, what the fuck," I said. I dumped the remainder into my mouth, not even bothering to use my hands. I had finished the entire bag in four minutes.

I felt repulsed that I had succumbed to my body's basic needs. Soon after that, I began purging. By senior year, my disordered eating had become so blatant that one day I logged on to our home computer and checked my email to find a note from my mother. Like me, she apparently needed the internet to have conversations that were too hard to have in person. There was a link to a Yahoo! article about the warning signs of anorexia. Below the link were the words:

I think you have a lot of these. I love you.

I closed the article and deleted the email.

My mom wasn't the only one who said something. My AP US history teacher kept me after class one day. After commenting on my thinness and paleness, she said, "You can always talk to me if something's not right." Before senior winter formal, my group of friends and our dates gathered with all the parents in our living room for photos. Natalie's mom was tall with beautiful brown chestnut hair. She had grown up in New York City and was very elegant. I overheard her as she leaned in to my mother's ear and said, "It takes one to know one."

Eventually, my mom worked up the nerve to discuss it with me. Over tears, she implored that I see a local doctor who specialized in disordered eating. It wasn't hard for her to convince me. I knew I needed help. One night, I stood in front of the bathroom mirror and looked at my body. I was no longer getting my period. I looked grotesque, like a statue. But I thought I looked oddly beautiful too. *Help me, God*, I wrote in my journal that night. *Fuck. What happened? Where have I gone? Who am I? I do not recognize myself.*

After just one meeting, the doctor recommended I seek residential live-in care. It was essential that I be separated from the routines of my disordered eating and get out of Fairfield County. My high school granted me a leave of absence, and I spent two months at a residential treatment facility in Florida. When I returned home, one of the first things I did was change my AIM profile to the serenity prayer. This was to reflect my new identity: someone in recovery from disordered eating.

This was also the first thing I said when I introduced myself to people upon arriving at college in Philadelphia. Most just gave me a weird look, unsure how to respond. I didn't yet know how to separate my recovery from other parts of my life. My doctor back home had notified the college's health department that I was in recovery, so I had to go to the campus nurse each week to be weighed. And I was still following the treatment protocol of food journaling, tracking everything I ate, and making sure I was getting enough of every category: grains, dairy, fruit, vegetables, fat, and protein.

But I wasn't supposed to keep tracking, not since I'd reached my target weight range. The whole point with tracking was to get to a healthy place where you could let go of it. But all around me were dorm-room mini fridges stocked with junk food like pizza rolls and red Solo cups full of sugary booze like Bacardí Razz. I would have loved to indulge in all of that carefree, but I wasn't there yet. In my mini fridge were whole-grain lavash flat wraps, peanut butter, Fage yogurt, trail mix, Sabra hummus, and carrots. And I was moderate with my drinking, which left me feeling alone and ostracized from my classmates.

In my isolation and with unrestricted access to my very own laptop, I found increasing solace in blogs about food and health. *Kath Eats Real Food* was one of my favorites. Kath lived in North Carolina. She ran 5Ks on the weekends, visited local breweries with her husband, and wore high-coverage bathing suits and modest dresses for weekend adventures to Charlottesville. Her view of food and exercise seemed balanced. Every morning around nine, she'd post a recap of her run along with a photo of her daily oatmeal. This wasn't your standard bowl of bland oats; hers were abundant and mouthwatering. She'd have a big bowl of them—sometimes chocolate or berry flavored—and then add a generous swirl of peanut butter on a spoon. She wrote about how she ate it, keeping the peanut butter on the spoon and dipping it in the oats so that she'd get a little bit of peanut butter in each bite. She'd update her blog usually two more times each day, being sure to include every single thing that crossed her lips, down to the exact amount. She'd photograph her plate with a caption that read: two bites of pita, scoop of Greek yogurt onion dip, 5. oz of chardonnay. Now, of course, I realize how easily this kind of food tracking can become an all-consuming habit—even if the person doing it seems wholesome. But at the time, I dreamed of being like her one day. I dreamed of allowing myself a weekend donut from the local farmer's market. But my eighteen-year-old brain, still fresh in recovery from her eating disorder, relished in reading what other women ate, *down to the crumb*. I found a bunch of other blogs through Kath's. I followed a community of women in their twenties who loved exercising and feeding their bodies well, who were passionate about the same things I was. Someone posted about a limited-edition gingerbread-flavored Clif Bar around the holidays, so I ordered a box from this website I'd just heard of called Amazon. Within a week, 150 Clif Bars arrived at my college dorm. I did not realize Amazon sold most of their items in massive quantities (bulk only) at the time. I ate Iced Gingerbread Clif Bars for the next eight months.

I loved reading these blogs, but I couldn't find one about a girl in college who was also new to recovery from an eating disorder. So I decided to make my own.

Using the free blogging platform WordPress, I signed up for the blog name *Philabundance of Life*, a kitschy mix of the affirmations I'd learned at treatment and my college town, Philadelphia. I knew exactly what to write for my first post. I started typing, introducing myself, sharing my story of the last few years of getting pulled out of high school and going to treatment. I finished it in two hours and pressed publish. Over the course of a few days, it had a few visits.

All the blogs at this time were connected through a top-ten recommendations list that appeared on each blog's home page. You could comment on any blogs you liked, which would automatically link to your own. The more you commented, the more eyes you got on your content. I commented a lot and posted even more.

Every morning, I posted my own dorm-room version of Kath's oatmeal bowl: one or two packs of instant Quaker maple and brown sugar oats and a packet of Smucker's peanut butter that I'd stockpiled from the cafeteria. Then I'd share a story or a few paragraphs of reflections on what I was struggling with: fall break, not fitting into the school culture, or going out to eat at a "scary" restaurant. Soon, I changed my blog's name to *For the Love of Peanut Butter*. With a clearer title, my blog grew even faster. By Christmas break, my website was getting over 230,000 views per month.

One time, I got an email from a reader: Can I send you an engraved spoon? I responded with my mailing address, and a few days later I received a homemade engraved spoon with the words INSERT PEANUT BUTTER HERE. It was so thoughtful. The blogging community was like that. We recommended products to each other and kept tabs on each other's day-to-day lives. People posted about pregnancy, sick relatives, divorce, and career changes. I had what I considered a real online community of friends. For Valentine's Day, I had the idea to organize a gift exchange among my mostly female readership. Over two hundred participants submitted their addresses to me, and I randomly matched them with someone else to send a gift to, like a Secret Santa for Valentines. I spent hours at my computer every night for weeks organizing this event. It went semi-viral, and everyone posted on their blogs what their "Cupid" had sent them, sometimes from across the country. My Cupid sent me organic popcorn, coffee beans, chocolates, and fresh fruit.

My blog depicted a young girl fully in recovery from disordered eating, but in reality, my recovery was extremely volatile. I was struggling to avoid purging and kept dropping below my target weight during weigh-ins at the college nurse's office. Instead of focusing on homework, I was focused on food and my weight. When I wasn't at a weigh-in or therapy, I was spending my time blogging about food and recovery or reading other people's blogs about food and recovery. My whole life was centered around food and recovery.

A popular blog with a massive readership reached out to interview me about my recovery and life in college. It was a go-to resource for young women, covering everything from sorority life and alcohol culture to the best book bags for looking cute on campus.

I said yes. The piece caused a massive influx of new readers. I got hundreds of emails from young girls struggling with disordered eating. I spent all my free time responding to their messages, glued to my computer for hours. I wrote back to the girls and their parents, telling them *It gets better!* and *Recovery is so worth it*, only to restrict my own calories that same day and go to bed with a growling stomach.

In the interview, I was identified by my real name, but I didn't worry about the consequences of having my name tied to such a personal interview, or what it would be like to have my story shared on another website that was not mine. I never showed my face in any of my blog posts or even shared where I went to school, which kept a level of anonymity I enjoyed. A few girls on campus discovered my blog, which I only found out by reading a comment under one of my blog posts that said, I saw you on campus today!

I remember feeling disheartened and a little embarrassed. I loved my online life, but I didn't want it to blend into my real life. Today, if a college kid is big on social media, they'd likely be adored and envied for it. But back then, being well-known online just meant you were a loser who didn't have any real friends. The few I did have were hurt that I hadn't confided my secret to them. My blog was like my secret personal diary, and I felt a little ashamed that strangers who could identify me in the real world had access to my deepest struggles. The boundary between my online world and real life had blurred, and I wasn't sure how to navigate it.

I started experiencing a depression so deep that I was afraid to leave my room. My mom, worried, picked me up early for Easter break. She took me to the doctor, who prescribed me Lexapro. Within two weeks, I noticed an improvement in my outlook and mood. I noticed the slightest tinge of happiness and I began looking forward to the future again. The long, dark Philly winter was lifting and spring was in full bloom.

I started to socialize more at school—going to parties and making Target runs with friends. One beautiful afternoon, I sat with some friends on a hill in front of the cafeteria. Shadowed by a grove of willows, we ate "Hawk wraps," the school's official sandwich: pita, fried chicken, tomato, onion, pickles, lettuce, and special sauce. I sat on my backpack and bit into the juicy wrap, relishing the salty flavors as pickle juice dripped down my hands and forearms. Below me, a group played Frisbee on the lawn.

I was so excited to be experiencing the real world and interacting with physical people. For the first time since starting college, I felt like I was truly enjoying the experience—because I was finally a part of it. I was no longer content spending hours a day on my blog, stuck in my ten-by-eight dorm room.

I wanted to be free from having to photograph, write about, and post my breakfast every day. I didn't want to think about food, especially oatmeal, anymore. I was glad that my blog had managed to help some people, but now I wanted to look out for myself. I wanted to be normal.

It took a few days to find the resolve, but I knew what I had to do. There was a moment of apprehension about my decision, but I saw no other choice. I didn't even warn my readers, say goodbye, or message any of the blog friends I'd made to let them know.

One day, I just opened my blog's settings, scrolled all the way to the bottom, and clicked "delete."

Are you sure? This is a permanent action.

Yes, I clicked.

I still had Facebook. And I was in the midst of discovering Tumblr, where I kept track of then niche celebrities like Sky Ferreira, Cory Kennedy, and Bebe Zeva. But that part would be just goofy and fun, just like Instagram was in the beginning.

The first photo[1] I uploaded to Instagram was in 2011, right before my senior year of college. I had just gotten an iPhone 4 through a free upgrade, downloaded the app everyone was talking about, and picked the username @holydances—after my favorite Beach House song.

It was a photo from a few months earlier when I was studying abroad in London. I'm at a flea market, looking at a piece of jewelry as the vendor holds it up for me. It's painfully 2011: My short hair is pinned to the side with a bobby pin. My eye makeup is heavy. I'm wearing a flannel, Levi's cutoffs over black tights, a maroon leather jacket, and a secondhand Dooney & Bourke cross-body purse.

I was using Instagram the only way I knew how to, like the scrapbook moments we'd put on Facebook, sharing highlights like nights out, summer trips, and studying abroad. I wasn't aware that this app was meant to be used in the moment. It was the first time I'd ever used a program where you could take a photo and post it, all without leaving the app.

The post got zero likes, and for a few years it remained that way. That was the first sign that my life was starting to change: when I began to receive notifications of likes and comments on that early post. My followers treated it like a game: Who could scroll back through my thousands and thousands of posts to the very first? I went all the way back.

Nobody was seeing the silly stuff I posted—or if they were, they weren't hitting the like button. Weird close-up selfies sticking my tongue out or making an angry face. A poem I wrote. The melted frozen yogurt at the bagel shop I worked at.

When I look back at my early IG posts, that's what makes me saddest: how innocent it all was at first. How innocent I was back then. How I could have fun posting a silly photo of bagel shop yogurt and not think twice about it.

Four

After college, I lived with my parents while working temp jobs to save up enough to move to New York City.

I found a girl on Craigslist and we signed a lease for a two-bedroom apartment on Thompson Street, just below Washington Square Park. The apartment was so small that I couldn't open my bedroom door fully without hitting the bed. There was no room for a dresser or even a nightstand. But it didn't matter. I had my own New York City apartment. And I had a job as an assistant to a floor of traders at a bank down on Wall Street.

Scrolling through Instagram one day, I saw a comment under a post by a band I followed. The username was @john_fromPoland. I went to the settings and typed *leefromamerica* into the "enter new username" section.

Congratulations! Your username has been changed.

I started posting more. My photos quickly phased out of being blurry and random. Now I was building an image of a twenty-two-year-old woman starting a life in New York. Mostly the posts were of nights out with old friends from college and new friends that I met at the club.

One night at Le Bain I met an older French man who was friends with the French DJ. He took me home to his big apartment in the Meatpacking District. In the morning, we shared a cigarette in bed, looking out the large glass windows at a visible sliver of the Hudson River.

"You poor thing," he said as he pushed my hair out of my face. "I pity you."

Another night at a club on the Lower East Side, I met a guy named Zev. Zev was in his late twenties and had lived in the city for about a decade. His apartment had been bought for him by his rich Westchester County father. After two weeks, I was spending almost every night there.

"You're the first girl I've ever slept with who didn't have a model's body," he told me. "You're a real woman, with a real body."

It didn't matter that my hips were size two. My anorexic self heard: *You're a fat, everyday kind of girl, and not like his ex.*

Zev's girlfriend before me was a model he'd scouted himself and helped sign to a big-time agency. She was now on every billboard around the city. She was eclectic, with piercings and purple hair, but still had a sweet, innocent look. Zev claimed, practically bragging, that she would wait outside his apartment, leaving voicemails begging him to take her back—all while we slept.

When we first started dating, Zev had more Instagram followers than me. Like myself and most people I knew, he checked the app voraciously. Whenever we went out, we took pictures of each other for our accounts: moody shots in a stairwell, out on a fire escape, up on a brownstone rooftop, or before a large bathroom mirror. We'd caption our images with just the right mix of mystery and lazy coolness. We both put in so much effort to make it seem like we didn't care. Once we launched our relationship on Instagram, we began cross-posting each other. Sometimes, a guy would comment on one of my posts, Wanna hang? Underneath his comment, Zev would respond, No.

He was possessive. "I'll protect you from all the rats in the city," he told me. "Here, people either want you for your looks, your money or your connections." But though Zev claimed to be cynical, he could become enraged when someone had more status and power than him. One time when he wasn't invited to a friend's VIP art party, he nearly punched the wall in anger.

"Are you fucking kidding me? I introduced Gary to Shawn, and now Gary is having this opening and inviting Shawn but not me? What a fucking retard!"

Zev's anger sometimes scared me. We went out six nights a week, drinking and taking molly, which Zev always dosed out to me. If I took molly without him, or took more than him, he'd yell at me over the club music, "What the fuck, Lee? You're such an untrustworthy slut!" The word scared me and reminded me of what my dad said when he walked in on me and Landon.

One morning, Zev and I were in bed. As he continued to sleep, I scrolled Instagram, liking every post under the hashtag #verboten, the popular Williamsburg club we'd left just a few hours before. It was my trick to growing followers. Hashtags were new to Instagram and people added them to every caption to file photos and participate in trends. You could search by hashtag, and everyone would always hashtag the clubs they went to. My hashtags often were: #forgtmenot, #disclosure, #maddecent, #mrsunday, #PLNYE, #output, #verboten nyc, and #eastvillage.

I'd dutifully search the club hashtag, like all the photos from the night prior, and then someone would see my like, go to my profile, catch a glance at my top row of photos, and decide to follow me. It was foolproof and it worked well.

I jumped out of my skin when I suddenly heard Zev ask what I was doing. He'd been watching me for ten minutes as I double-tapped my phone. "It's like you're in some meditative trance." I looked at the clock and was surprised to see I'd been doing it for ninety minutes, reaching my like-per-hour limit, then waiting for it to reset.

Zev grabbed my phone and threw it on the ground next to him, out of my reach. "Come here," he said, pulling me into his arms, smelling like tequila. But I didn't want to cuddle. I wanted to keep scrolling.

Five

My online persona continued to change. Now, instead of a young woman starting life in New York, I was curating the image[2] of a cool downtown girl: weekend excursions to the Instagram-friendly rainbow walls in Dumbo; photos at Soho House; at Zev's dad's apartment in Tribeca and their house in Rhode Island; of trips to LA and Coachella, mostly paid for by Zev. It was working. Soon I had more followers than he did. This annoyed Zev.

"It's 'cause you're a hot girl," he said. "That's why. Every guy just wants to fuck you."

I was not posting about my unglamorous job: I'd since left the bank and was now an assistant at a hedge fund. It was just me and the owner. That's it. He'd asked me to take a Series 7 test to begin trading, but I had absolutely no interest in finance. It was just the only job I had been able to get. I spent my days at my desk in the small Tribeca office, eating a sandwich from Cafe Clementine, listening to DJ sets, scrolling Instagram and Tumblr, and G-chatting with Zev. Finally, my boss fired me.

Zev encouraged me to apply for creative industry jobs—and to lead with my Instagram account in my emails. He might have been jealous of my follower count, but he was business savvy. He knew how much it would impress hiring managers if they saw my account, and knew my Instagram was better than any business card or résumé. It showed the image of the girl you'd want to work for your company: fun, carefree, stylish, and a frequent visitor to all the city's coolest cafés and restaurants.

Zev was right. I quickly picked up a temp job as a production assistant at the Calvin Klein New York Fashion Week show, and then another job producing pop-ups—well before that became common. Then one night I went to a Red Bull industry party. There, I saw Chris. Chris operated a series of buzzy restaurants around the Lower East Side and threw underground parties in secret warehouse locations, revealing the address on Twitter the day of. I'd seen him at parties or events with Zev. Now I sat down next to him and, after a few minutes of conversation, told him I was looking for a job. He gave me his card and said to email him. I did the next morning, signing it with @lee fromamerica.

The very next day, Chris offered me a role as the assistant to a new restaurant he was opening in SoHo.

"We'd love for you to join our team," he said. "Your Instagram is so cool, we could really use that kind of creativity here!"

I arrived on my first day at the restaurant job to construction workers coming in and out, dust barriers hung haphazardly, and contractors hammering and sawing. Chris, trying to onboard me, yelled over the noise. It was the period leading up to opening. It was hectic, but I loved it.

The chef was a Brooklyn native named Vinny who came in every day to test our menu items. He high-fived me and called me a rock star. It felt like we were building the coolest restaurant in Manhattan.

Everyone Chris hired was a personality—and if they weren't, he made them one. Did one of the chefs also paint on the side? He was now a "street artist." Did someone once get mentioned on a cooking website? They were now "award-winning." Did the hostess previously work for two days at Pastis and then get fired? We could still say she "left" her job at the esteemed restaurant to join our team. Because I'd spent one summer in college working on a farm, I was the in-house "farmer."

For our launch, Chris hired a videographer who'd done work at Nike to create a trendy video that had the energy of a Hypebeast promo. Slo-mo shots of Vinny selecting vegetables at the Union Square farmer's market and fish from a Chinatown stall were interspersed with interviews of us, our Instagram handles and misleading monikers flashing across the screen as a Sbtrkt song played in the background. Chris was building an image of this restaurant as a cool spot to eat staffed by cool people with cool credentials.

As Chris's assistant, I pitched the video out to *Grub Street*, *BuzzFeed*, CBS, *GMA*, and all of Chris's many press contacts. My job was not limited to PR. Depending on the day, I might be calling a plumber to fix a leak in the basement or giving a walk-through to editors at *Vogue* and other people from Chris's VIP contact list: celebrities, models, DJs, and socialites. I was their tour guide. Chris treated this list like it was the Holy Grail. If I even made so much as a spelling error in an email to one of these people, Chris—always cc'd—would come down to my coatroom office and say, "Lee, no more typos. Seriously, we can't let that happen." I'd been fired before, but this time I actually wanted to keep the job. It meant something to me.

Once the restaurant opened, we were constantly inviting in these VIPs for a comped meal. They'd post a photo, and we'd repost it on our Instagram, which I also handled. Since I had more followers than the restaurant, I promoted the restaurant on my personal Instagram too. I added the restaurant's handle to my bio and frequently posted updates like We're doing lunch service! and Weekend brunch now extended! The restaurant's account sometimes seemed as misleading as my own. We called ourselves farm-to-table and wrote a list of our "local farm purveyors" on the chalkboard walls, but we got much of our food delivered from Baldor.

I also started giving tours to people whose Instagrams were devoted to food and restaurants. This was a new thing—so new that the term "influencer" wasn't being used yet. But you couldn't call them "reviewers." They got a free meal in exchange for a post, and so they never wrote anything negative. Whatever they were called, they helped bring more people to the restaurant. Dedicated to growing my follower count, I always followed them, and they always followed me back.

Chris was the beneficiary of this quid pro quo in other ways. During New York Fashion Week, we were hired to cater backstage at Rebecca Minkoff's runway show. A few days later, he cc'd me on an email:

> Hey Rebecca Minkoff team! I loved the cross-body bag you sent me last year, but it's really tattered now. Can I get a new one?

A box soon arrived at the restaurant. Not only did it contain the bag of his choice, but a pair of shoes and the Rebecca Minkoff signature satchel had also been thrown in. I was learning a big lesson: If you were deemed worthy, you could get free stuff.

Better than that, you could get money.

Six months into my job, Chris asked me to reach out to sparkling water companies to sponsor an event we were hosting at the restaurant.

"Tell them that if they want to get involved, they need to pay us a thousand dollars. And Lee, if you get that 1K, I'll give you a cut of it. Two hundred dollars. Get that money!"

"What?!" I said. "Will they actually give us a thousand dollars to be at our event?"

"Hell yeah," Chris said. "Brands have all the money and marketing budgets."

I emailed a prominent sparkling water brand. I included the flyer to our event and names of expected VIP attendees. I told them they'd be the one and only sparkling water represented.

Within moments, I got a response.

We'd love to be a part of it! Thanks for asking! How much?

$1,000.

Got it. Where should we send the check?

I couldn't believe it. It was that easy. It was the fastest $200 I'd ever made in my life. I ran upstairs to tell Chris the good news.

"Hell yeah! See, Lee? We did it! We built something cool that brands want to be a part of. It's all about the *brand*."

Six

Zev and I were fighting more and more. He was upset that I was devoting so much time to my job. One night after a big fight and momentary breakup, an influential Scientologist filmmaker in his fifties was drinking at our restaurant's bar by himself. He asked me for my number. The next day, I was at a red-carpet event with him. I told Zev it was to help boost the profile of the restaurant: If people saw my name in the photo alongside the celebrity, they'd go to my Instagram page and see my link to the restaurant, which could help bring us more customers and press. Zev didn't believe me. Nor did he believe my denials to his constant accusations that I was fucking Chris. One night he went through my phone and saw a message to my friend in which I vented about his paranoia and possessiveness. He freaked out, grabbed my wrist, and twisted my arm hard. He didn't know that I had grown up breaking free of similar holds from my parents. I ripped my hand away and told him to never do it again.

The next day he came to me crying, apologizing, while still defending his actions.

"You weren't listening," he said. "You always do this."

He also started getting more demanding about sex. He loved

blow jobs and would wake me up and push my head down to his groin area despite my saying no.

"Please, baby," he'd whine in a baby voice. "I want to feel what it's like inside your mouth. I'm so good to you. Please."

I would always relent.

Though he would freak out if I even glanced in another guy's direction, he didn't feel so inhibited. He once said, "I can tell what a girl's vagina looks like by looking at her lips."

Then one night in his kitchen, he told me his model ex-girlfriend would be staying at his apartment for a week while he was out of town. When I told him how weird that was, he said, "You're so insecure! Why can't you relax? Most girls are chill with this, Lee!"

That was it. I could no longer contain the rage that had built up over the course of our relationship. I jabbed the bridge of his nose with my fingers, hard enough to send him stumbling into the fridge, his glasses cracking on impact. It didn't help. All it did was make my life feel even more out of control.

A few nights later, we went to dinner at Cafe Cluny, one of our favorites in the West Village. After we finished our tuna burgers, I could only focus on getting the food out of my stomach. I went to the bathroom and made myself purge for the first time in years.

Zev knew about my history. Zev and I did a lot of drugs and partied a lot, but we also both worked hard to stay slim. And when I got back to the table, he suspected what I'd done.

"You just threw up, didn't you?"

I nodded.

He grabbed my hands.

"Promise me, Lee," he said, looking deeply into my eyes, "that you will never make yourself throw up again." He looked on the brink of tears. I promised—and I've kept that promise ever since.

I wish I could say that was the moment we realized we weren't healthy for each other, that we decided it would be best for both of us to make a clean break, and that we did so with mutual respect and kindness. But the ending to our relationship was much messier and more drawn out. The cycle worsened: Zev would yell and scream at me and send me home in a fit of tears, I'd break up with him, he'd call me and beg for forgiveness, I'd take him back.

On the night of our final breakup, as I walked out of his apartment for good, the last words he ever said to me were: "You're such an Instagram whore. All you care about is likes. Just please don't fuck anybody I know."

Seven

After the breakup, I threw myself into the party scene.[3] I was going out almost every night of the week. After I left the restaurant, I'd go back to my apartment and change into my go-to club outfit: a cropped cartoon-print stretchy tank on top with Topshop black high-waisted hot shorts on the bottom. On my feet, I'd wear either a pair of Jeffrey Campbell daisy Litas or white high-top Converse if I was going to be dancing like crazy. I would text a couple guy friends who worked in finance and always had plenty of ketamine, coke, and molly—and would gladly share with girls. I'd meet them at a club with some of my girlfriends. Output, Verboten, and Marquee were some of our favorites. I could easily get us in. Thanks to the hospitality industry contacts I'd built through the restaurant—as well as the network of my own I'd built over Instagram—I was friends with most of the city's club owners, promoters, doormen, and staff. Once inside the club, I'd follow my own little drug-ridden routine. First, I'd put a few dabs of molly on my tongue, and then I'd sprinkle some into a water bottle. Molly water was my favorite drug. It was calorie-free, hydrating, and I could control how high I wanted to get. I knew it was entering my bloodstream when I started to feel a warm pulsing sensation deep in my core that traveled up toward my scalp and back down, pooling between my legs. Within minutes, it would reach my fingertips and my whole body would feel electric. I would go out onto the dance floor and not leave until four or five in the morning, which was when I'd usually go home with a stranger. Sometimes a man, and sometimes a woman. I'd been curious and wanted to explore that side of myself.

In the past when I'd dance with girls at the club, Zev would throw his arm around me, marking his territory. Now, I was on my own, and free to follow whatever impulse came up.

I loved molly, but the comedown was intense. The depression the next day was debilitating. I'd often stay in bed until noon, feeling the walls closing in, anxious and paranoid with a sense of doom coming at me from all four corners. I attempted to manage it with coke and cigarettes. And Instagram. For hours I'd zone out in a trancelike state as I edited my photos and scrolled Instagram's Popular page.

At this point in 2014, everyone in New York City was on Instagram. My friends and I used it to keep in touch with each other, and a few brands were starting to use it too. Instagram had its own filters like Mayfair and Valencia, but I loved using an app called Afterlight for more customizable color toning and textures. I always found time for editing my night out, no matter how dead I felt inside.

Then, I'd go to work and do it all over again the next night.

Chris and I went down to Miami for Miami Music Week. The goal was to continue to grow our network and build interest in the restaurant. It was nonstop partying—from afternoons at the Red Bull Guest House to client dinners, followed by nights at clubs like the Edition, Soho Beach House, and the Broken Shaker, and ending with beach afterparties that stretched into dawn. On the third day, I was so exhausted that I skipped dinner out to get a little downtime in my hotel room. Then I got a text from Chris:

Lee, where r u? client is here, plz show them a good time.

I dragged myself out of bed and down to the Gale on Collins Avenue. I saw one of Chris's friends, a French DJ-curator-creative. "Do you have molly?" I screamed into his ear over the loud bass. If I was going to stay up, I needed something.

"Yes," he screamed back with a smile. "Only if you dance with me."

"Okay," I yelled.

He produced something in a bag. I wet my finger with my tongue and put the grayish powder in my mouth. Euphoria ensued within minutes, but anxiety was right behind it. My neck started itching, and I felt a dark paranoia. I realized what he had given me wasn't molly. I started hallucinating. "Did I just take meth?" I asked myself aloud while staring at my big black eyes in the club's grimy basement mirror. I didn't want to know, and made sure to never see that man again.

During this time, I wasn't eating much due to all the drugs and cigarettes—maybe a little quinoa for dinner to get something in my stomach—and I'd become almost as skinny as when I'd gone to the treatment facility. I also had perpetual "molly eyes" in many of my Instagram photos—the pupils taking over the irises and making my eyes a ghoulish black.

Later that summer, I ran into an old friend from high school at Governors Ball. She texted another high school friend of mine telling her how terrible I looked. That friend in turn texted my mom, who called me and expressed her concern. My mom had recently joined Instagram and was following me.

"Lee, I'm worried."

"Mom, what are you worried about? I'm fine!" I cooed.

I even started doing coke at work. Chris knew but didn't mind. He loved how much I went out. I was going backstage at concerts and festivals and would often invite the DJs to the restaurant the following night. One night, after partying until four a.m., my friends and I walked from Meatpacking down to the Seaport. Drunk and desperate to pee, I led us to the restaurant, unlocked the doors with my emergency key, and we used the bathrooms, jumped around on the banquettes, did lines of coke on the tables, then headed back out to watch the sunrise.

One night I met one of my finance friends at Verboten. This guy always carried two bags: a red one for coke and a blue one for molly. I asked for coke, putting the outside of my hand out, thumb and pointer finger together to create a compression bowl between the two fingers. He sprinkled a little bit on my hand.

"More!" I yelled.

He added some more to the pile. I put it to my nose and inhaled. Within seconds, the music was wobbling, and time, or my recognition of it, stopped altogether. I felt my brain shut off.

Everything went black.

Moments or hours later, I heard my name.

"Lee!" Their voice was muffled, as if underwater. I regained consciousness slightly, enough to realize I was sitting down on the side of the dance floor, slouched over on a banquette.

"Lee, are you okay?"

"Oh my God, you guys, she doesn't look good."

"Oh my God, you guys, she's in a K-hole!"

I could hear these people yelling, but I couldn't move or respond.

"What happened?"

"She took too much K!"

Eventually, after about an hour, I was able to get back on my feet. As soon as I did, I went to find the finance guy I'd come with.

"I need more drugs," I said. "And make sure it's coke this time!"

I snorted a mountain of actual coke and got right back to my night.

The next morning, unsure of how I'd gotten back to my apartment, surprised and relieved that no one was sharing my bed, I realized something had to change. If it didn't, I'd either end up in rehab or dead. As with my usual hangover ritual, I reached for my phone and started scrolling.

I stumbled on the account of a woman named Loni Jane. This was my first time seeing any type of "influencer" content on Instagram. Her page was just like the blogs I kept up with in college, but in short-form content.

She lived in Australia with her husband and son and had perfectly straight ombre-blonde hair, earthy green eyes, and a year-round tanned and toned body. Her diet was 100 percent vegan and raw—photos of which she shared on her grid along with plunges into impossibly turquoise waters, her impeccably designed apartment, and her faceless, muscular husband.

I wanted that life.

I dragged myself out of bed, pulled on clothes, and walked to Chinatown to a newly opened healthy takeaway spot called Dimes. In a few years, Dimes would get so popular that the neighborhood would be named Dimes Square. But at the time it was only known to people in our particular scene, a chic lunch spot on a random triangle in Chinatown. I ordered their kohlrabi salad, and before I ate it, I posted a photo of it with the hashtag #notsaddesklunch. It got seventy-six likes.

Eight

When Zev had said that the only reason my Instagram was growing faster than his was because guys wanted to fuck me, he wasn't entirely wrong. As I'd realized with those early experiences on my first desktop computer, sex was always inextricable from life online. Instagram was no different. I followed women like Loni Jane and Ellen Fisher because I thought they were hot and intriguing. They were selling the healthy lifestyle, but there was sensuality oozing from every photo to draw people in.

Through their pages, I stumbled upon another account called @freeleethebananagirl. Another ombre blonde, Freelee posed alongside her big tits and impossibly toned stomach in an unspecified jungle in Australia. Through her, I learned about the specific diets of these hot Australian women, namely #801010, #rawtill4, and #banana island.

#801010 was in reference to the diet that prescribed 80 percent carbs, 10 percent protein, and 10 percent fat. I quickly adopted it. Due to my treatment experience, I was drawn to simple calculations of food intake. I loved how all the guesswork of what to eat was removed.

#rawtill4 was the way to implement this diet: You ate a raw breakfast and lunch, and for dinner, you were allowed cooked food. This especially appealed to me as someone living in a tiny New York City apartment where cooking was a challenge. I had smoothies for breakfast, salad for lunch, and quinoa topped with poached eggs and canned marinara sauce for dinner.

And #bananaisland was a method of "detoxing" the body, in which you spent a long weekend eating just bananas. Followers of the diet claimed it helped with decision fatigue and weight loss. I couldn't deny that eating solely bananas for as long as I could sounded attractive, weird, and aligned with our "primitive desires." Considering I was eating a mostly raw, vegan diet—and no longer drinking—I wasn't sure exactly what I was supposed to be detoxing from. But I tried it one weekend all the same.

I went to Chinatown, where I knew I could buy cheap bananas in bulk. I bought twenty bananas, thinking it would last me three days. On the first day, I ate two bananas for breakfast, four for lunch, and five for dinner. I loved peeling each banana and watching the peels pile up on my apartment's desk, which also served as a dining room table. It felt empowering and simple—a "monomeal" as the Instagram vegans called it. Why had we as a society made everything so complicated? Anytime I was hungry, I could just reach for bananas. I didn't have to think.

The next morning, I made "nice cream." I put four frozen bananas, some cinnamon powder, and vanilla bean into my Vitamix. Because there was no liquid, the Vitamix jolted around violently trying to grind up the frozen banana chunks. Using the tamper and all the muscle power I could muster, I continuously pressed the bananas down toward the blade to get it smooth. The end result was unbearably sweet, almost metallic, thanks to the ethylene of a super-ripe banana. By lunch, I was feeling sick from all the bananas. It took me an hour to eat two bananas, I chewed so slowly, wincing and gagging as I swallowed. I could feel a canker sore developing in my mouth. All in all, I lasted a day and a half on Banana Island.

The women I followed also posted photos of themselves exercising. Though I didn't have the crystalline ocean to swim in or lush trails to hike, at least I could run. I started running every day before work, and sometimes even after work. I'd run through the nighttime streets of Manhattan, briefly leaving the curb to pass doddering girls in towering heels who had been me just a few months before. I built up my endurance one mile at a time, until I was running for hours.

I was always starving after my runs and loved making myself a smoothie. One morning, still sweaty and a bit shaky from low blood sugar, I made a smoothie with avocado, banana, coconut, kale, and some water. It was so thick, I decided to pour it into a bowl from Anthropologie. (Even though my small apartment didn't allow for much cooking, I still made sure to have cool dishware.) I sprinkled on some toppings: a mixture of nuts, seeds, and some raw granola that I'd made in the food processor from dates and coconut. Then I took a picture[4] of it and uploaded it to Instagram with the caption:

#Avocado #banana #kale #acaibowl with #leefromamericagranola, #rawcoconutbutter and hella #flaxseeds. Dating my **@vitamix** basically.

The likes and a comment instantly poured in:

Can you make this for me eerrrrday **@leefromamerica** please?!?

A few days later, I posted another bowl, this time with defined lines of toppings including kiwi, crushed pistachio, coconut shreds, chia, and cacao nibs.

Girl, u be killlin' em' like BEEN

So tumblr

I want to make this tomorrow

Looks delicious

People started tagging their friends in my comments to share the posts.

The first smoothie bowl was born.

Maybe someone had posted a smoothie bowl before me, but I had never seen one, and I zealously followed everyone on "Healthy Instagram." Until then, people either posted acai bowls or oat bowls with lots of toppings. A smoothie bowl with a bright green, pink, or sunny yellow base was unheard of. Due to the popularity of that first post, I started regularly posting smoothie bowls, inventing new flavors as I went along: peanut butter and chocolate, red velvet with beets, carrot cake, caramel swirl, blueberry maple coconut cream. I decorated them with precision, placing the nut and seed toppings in neat little rows, perfectly uniform. I photographed them from above, making sure each ingredient was totally in focus, like you could reach through the screen and take a bite. My secret was plenty of good natural light. It was impossible to scroll past my smoothie bowls. Each design was like a mandala, hypnotic, demanding attention. The only person who wasn't enamored with them was my roommate. She did not appreciate all the loud smoothie-making.

Though my roommate and I weren't getting along, I was making a lot of new friends though Instagram. Some of them I'd meet IRL. We'd take Beyond Sushi to the High Line or grab avocado toast at this bright new Aussie café called Two Hands, a place that practically begged to be documented. Each meetup was marked with a photo of the two of us to share on Instagram, always making sure to tag each other and include a heartfelt caption about how special it was to meet up with like-minded women who also put their health and wellness first. It was the dawn of the girlboss.

In another effort to grow my followers, I'd travel to the city's various farmer's markets and independent grocers who specialized in alternative ingredients like watermelon radishes, maca, mesquite powder, and chia seeds. I'd take a photo of my finds and post it with a little story about the shop, making sure to tag them.

I had made granola at different points in my life, and it was always a hit. Every time I shared it on Instagram—cheekily calling it "Granolee"—my followers would ask if I'd sell it to them. I debuted it on Instagram and sold a few jars but quickly gave it up. Instagram was still just a silly hobby, and I already had a full-time job. Though not for much longer.

Nine

Since Chris had tapped into everyone in New York who could help bring attention to the restaurant, he started sending me to LA to do the same out there—with the aim of an eventual West Coast expansion. I'd stay in West Hollywood, and just before dawn I'd run up Runyon Canyon. Once at the top, I'd ask a stranger to take my photo just as the sun came up over the horizon behind me. What the photos never showed were the moments just before, when I was gasping for air with my hands on my knees and close to vomiting from the trail's nearly ninety-degree incline. The light in LA was so incredible for photos. I continued to follow and study influencers' posts as well as others who were joining the growing "Healthy Instagram" community. I added all their same hashtags—#raw, #rawvegan, #rawtill4, #vegansofig, #veganfoodshare, #cleanfoodporn—to every single one of my posts. And my follower count steadily grew, reaching around three thousand. I loved the community, inspiration, and was endlessly intrigued by how these women had devoted their whole lives to living healthy.

But I noticed one thing. All these women looked the same: tall, thin, and model-like. Zev's ex-girlfriend, basically. None of them looked like me: a 5'6" slightly goofy and awkward girl from suburban Connecticut. And they all took themselves so seriously. None of them had my sense of humor. I realized that if I could be funnier and show real sides of my personality, it would help set me apart.

I was right.

I posted photos of myself in cute outfits (leather Maje motorcycle jacket, oversized Zara scarf, American Apparel tennis skirt, perforated black Vans leather slip-ons) next to a brick wall with graffiti that read I LOVE YOU. It's true I do, I wrote in the caption.

I also posted my stained red hands after peeling steamed beets with the caption beet murdering.

I started to let people into my life, posting my whereabouts, schedule, and personality. It's my peanut butter acai smoothie versus this seagull, who's gonna win? my caption read below a photo of my beach smoothie while on business in Miami.

But my smoothie bowl posts continued to get the most likes. Every morning, I'd wake up at 5:45, work out at the gym or go for a run, take a shower, make a smoothie bowl, decorate it, photograph it, and then walk to the restaurant. I'd write the caption once I got to work and post it at exactly ten a.m., which I learned from trial and error was the best time for engagement—I assumed because, like me, that was when people were just getting to work, and they were quickly bored at their jobs and looking to procrastinate. I followed this routine for months.

One trip to LA, I visited Sqirl, a breakout restaurant I'd been seeing on Instagram known for their crunchy rice bowls and loaded avocado toast on freshly baked brioche. I stood in a line that stretched down the block and around the corner. Soon joining the line behind me was a cute guy with a black Lab.

When I reached the counter twenty minutes later, I ordered the avocado toast, the crunchy rice bowl, and an iced matcha with almond milk.

"You gotta get the lava cake too," said the cute guy behind me. I turned and locked in on his inky brown eyes. Before I could answer, Sqirl's owner came out from the kitchen, tapping the man at the register.

"You're Lee, right?" she said.

I nodded.

"The lava cake is on us!"

It was the first time I'd ever been recognized for my Instagram. I exhaled, trying to play it cool in front of the cute guy. Apparently, he was friendly with the chef. She hugged him and, clearly picking up on the vibe, introduced us. His name was Tate. We shook hands and I went outside to sit at one of the sidewalk tables to wait for my order. Tate had just been grabbing a coffee and a pastry to go. On his way out, he stopped by my table.

"Where do you live?" he asked.

"New York. You?"

"Downtown. I've got a restaurant in the Arts District." He was too modest to tell me then, but I would later learn he was a highly regarded chef—not yet thirty and already the recipient of multiple prestigious awards.

"What are you doing in LA?" he asked.

"I'm here for work," I said. "I'm also in the restaurant industry." We chatted a little bit about my restaurant, which he hadn't heard of.

"That's why I'm here," I said.

"Well, clearly you are good at your job," he said, returning my smile.

He asked me to dinner. I said yes. He asked for my phone number. I gave it to him. Then he asked for my Instagram.

"Lee From America," I said. He looked me up.

"Whoa," he said. "What are these?"

"Smoothie bowls," I said.

"Damn," he said. "People love 'em!"

"I guess they do!"

I beamed with pride. Instagram would now get me lava cakes and dates.

Ten

One morning, I was scrolling through the comments of my pumpkin pie smoothie bowl post.

> Yo girl! Looove your stuff. I write for the @freepeople blog & would love to collab if you're interested. Do you have an email I could reach you at? 🌸

I couldn't believe it. Free People had been one of my favorite clothing brands for years. I loved their carefree boho looks. The comment was three days old. What if I'd lost my chance? It was ten p.m. They had provided an email address. I sent them a message:

> Oh my god. How did I miss this? I'd love to do it!

The next morning, I sat at work, unable to focus, continuously checking my email to see if Free People had responded. Finally, at eleven a.m., a reply came in.

Hey! Definitely still interested in featuring you!

Their idea was a feature on their blog titled "In the Kitchen with Lee." It would be an interview and photo shoot at my apartment centered around my smoothie bowls.

We set up the date, and I got to work drafting what the smoothie bowl would look like. With a pencil and notebook, I sketched and diagrammed until I was satisfied. Each topping was placed even more meticulously than usual.

I spent nearly as much time choosing my outfit for the shoot. I settled on a pine-green Zara sweater, gray Urban Outfitters skinny jeans, and black suede Steve Madden wood-heeled boots. Per my instructions, the Free People photographer arrived just before eleven a.m., when the apartment received the best light of the day. We rolled my desk into the living area, where the sofa was, to give the illusion that I had a large, bright kitchen and not a windowless nook that could fit either the coffee machine or the Vitamix, not both. As I made the smoothie, the photographer moved all around me, taking shots.[5]

When it came time to decorate the top of the smoothie bowl, my heart started racing. I felt pressure—now I was doing this in front of an audience, and for the press! I leaned over the chopping board, slicing the banana into quarter-inch pieces, fanning them out so they wouldn't sink to the bottom of the bowl, just as I'd taught myself. As I delicately spread the seeds by hand, I tried not to mind the sweat running from my armpits down my sides. When the smoothie bowl was finished, it was exactly how I'd envisioned it.

A week later, Free People sent me the questions for the interview. When I returned them, I asked if in addition to running it on their blog they would also post it on their Instagram (1.6 million followers) and tag me.

They said they'd have to discuss it with their social media team.

A few days later, they responded and said they would. They also asked if I had a website they should link to. Immediately, I bought the domain Leefromamerica.com for $35. I synced my Tumblr to my new site so that I'd have some posts for any new visitors to peruse. I wasn't blogging much anymore, but it was better than nothing. I added an About page, my email address, and a picture of myself from the Free People shoot. I beamed with pride.

When the piece went live, I was crossing West 3rd Street on my way to work. Barely looking up to spot cars, I scrolled through it. It looked amazing—the deep purple of the bowl and each individual seed clarified through the photographer's professional lens.

Then it happened. My notifications buzzed, one after the other.

@abbygirl334 started following you.

@healthygirl_ started following you.

@jans2424 and 5 others started following you.

@sunflowersweetie5122 and 25 others started following you.

One hundred new followers. Three hundred new followers. Six hundred new followers.

Tears streaming down my face, I called my mom.

"Mom, oh my God, I've gone viral."

"Oh, Lee, I'm so happy for you, sweetie! That's so cool!"

When I got to work, I couldn't concentrate on anything. I just kept refreshing the Instagram app, looking at my follower count tick up by multiples of one hundred and trying to reply to all the comments.

Are you going to write a cookbook?

How do you cook this?!

What kind of @vitamix do you have?!

"Lee." Chris stood there at my desk, catching me by surprise. "I saw the piece. How come you didn't mention the restaurant in it?"

"Oh, I—I—"

"Come on, Lee, next time you do press, you gotta mention us. We gotta help each other out. Whenever I get press, I always mention the restaurant."

Chris walked away from my desk.

Fuck this place, I thought. In the months since meeting Tate at Sqirl, we texted every day, and I stayed with him the couple times I'd been back to LA. He told me he couldn't make it work unless we lived in the same city. I'd been considering it more and more, and now I was convinced it was time. That night, I started searching for apartments in LA. And before I went to bed, I refreshed the Instagram app one last time. In just eight hours, I'd doubled the following it had taken me three years to build.

I'd told my parents about wanting to move to LA. They didn't understand why I was quitting a stable job in hopes of chasing a career that didn't even exist yet. They had no idea about the potential that I saw in this app and my work. I promised I'd take care of myself and if things didn't work out, I could always move back to New York. I'd told my dad I needed to move somewhere warmer for work so I could make smoothies and exercise more.

"I'm thinking either Australia or LA," I said.

"Why don't you try LA first?" he responded. "It's closer."

Eleven

I had started encountering the term "influencer" before I left New York, but—as with so much in New York—it was always with an above-it-all mixture of sarcasm, mockery, and disdain. I'd overhear conversations like "What is this influencer bullshit? Whatever happened to wanting to be an artist?" I agreed that "influencer" was embarrassingly self-aggrandizing, and I wasn't about to describe myself that way—even though I probably had enough followers to technically qualify. But I did think there was some artistry to my smoothie bowls. What I was creating was clearly connecting with people and generating hundreds of passionate responses at a time. Wasn't that the kind of connection art was all about? Also, I had met plenty of people during my time at the restaurant and club scene who called themselves "artists" but seemed too busy partying to actually create anything. They dressed well and hung out at all the best parties, but they were just scenesters. These were people like Zev, whose parents paid for their apartments and made sure they didn't have to worry about something so trivial as a job. These were the people who had come through the financial crisis unscathed and maybe even better off. These were the people who could scoff at the prospect of something so demeaning as trying to scrape together rent money from whatever hustle they could find, including social media. I didn't have that luxury. I moved to LA with a single suitcase containing a few changes of clothes, my Vitamix, and my entire savings: $3,000.

I leased a Honda Fit because it offered the best gas mileage, and I took a sublet in a Silver Lake two-bedroom. The other tenant was named Josie. Originally from Oregon, she practiced Ashtanga, was in nutrition school, and claimed an anti-inflammatory diet had healed her Lyme disease. We'd already exchanged Instagram handles and quickly realized our shared interests.

"You're an influencer." She said it so casually to me, without any scorn—not as a question, but as a statement of fact.

"I guess I am," I said.

"Yeah. I went semi-viral a few months ago, and after thinking about it, decided that path is not for me. I'm going to get my nutritionist degree and open up a healthy café in Echo Park."

In that moment, I realized Josie and I would be taking two very distinct paths: hers, nutrition and hospitality; mine, digital and building my community. I felt a level of shame that I was choosing this path; hers seemed more "pure."

After the success of the Free People post, brands started reaching out asking if they could send me their products. Most were small businesses related to smoothies, such as almond butter or freeze-dried berry powder. I said yes to it all. I'd also be proactive. I'd go for a browse at Erewhon for things I wanted to try, then email or DM the company and ask them to send products to me in exchange for a mention. They always did: sauerkraut, goat's milk yogurt, granola, nut butter, frozen coconut meat. Anything I wanted in the health and wellness world I could most likely get for free. And I knew I could make money from it too.

I remembered my experience with the restaurant and the sparkling water sponsorship. When a matcha brand emailed me asking if I'd like to try some of their product, I responded:

Sure. And for $75, I'll incorporate it into a recipe and post it on my blog and Instagram.

They wrote back: Where can we send the check?

There was no contract. And unlike now, there were no FTC guidelines or requisite #ad hashtag. They just sent me the check and I posted their powder the following week. My first sponsored post was done. This was different from when I received gifted products, which did not always require me to sign a contract or post anything specific, but the implication was that it would benefit the brand if I did.

After that, I began organizing my entire life around getting content for Instagram. My followers were interested in how my move to LA was going, and I closely documented it, upping my post frequency to twice a day. My smoothie bowls remained my top-performing posts.

One day, Josie watched me as I made one. She had her own Vitamix. Unlike my New York apartment, her countertops were big enough for both to sit side by side. She would make a smoothie for breakfast but otherwise adhered to a diet of pasture-raised beef, bone broth, and dark leafy greens. There was hardly any room for me in the freezer with all the frozen organ meat.

"That's a lot of banana," she said.

"What do you mean?" I asked over the noisy whir of the machine.

"Well, banana spikes your blood sugar. It's got tons of fructose in it, and when fructose enters the bloodstream, it metabolizes into the liver, turning into glucose, where it often gets stored as excess fat. You didn't know bananas contain tons of sugar?"

I looked at Josie blankly, holding my Vitamix tamper, mouth suddenly dry.

"That's why my smoothies contain things like berries, kale, bee pollen, and coconut water," she said. "No bananas."

I immediately decided to follow her advice and eliminated bananas from my diet. But I still kept them in the smoothie bowls I made and photographed each morning. Without bananas, the bowl wouldn't be thick enough to support the pretty toppings for Instagram. After posting them to Instagram, I'd usually throw them out or bring them to my yoga studio for someone else to eat.

Twelve

While LA might have been more receptive to the idea of an influencer than New York, it was a lot harder to meet people and make friends than it had been back East. I had heard this before I moved—that everyone living all spread out and having to drive in miserable traffic thwarted the kinds of spontaneous and serendipitous encounters that came from taking the subway and walking everywhere.

My relationship with Tate—or whatever it was—fizzled before my move. Once I told him I was coming, he started to pull away. The night before my flight, I saw he had posted a picture of him and a girl hiking in Topanga Canyon. I didn't even bother to text him about it. We simply were never in touch again.

Eager for any opportunity to meet people, I quickly said yes when a hip boutique hotel in the idyllic mountain town of Ojai, about two hours north of LA, offered to let me stay there free for a weekend in exchange for posts about the hotel. The first night, the hotel had live music and a Santa Barbara food truck serving oysters. I was chatting with a few local girls around my age when a man with long hair sat down next to me. His name was Joseph. He was covered in tattoos, wore a structured flat-brim hat, and had the deep tan of someone who spent most of their life outdoors. I was instantly attracted to him.

"See that Airstream back there?" he said, nodding to a silver camper seated next to the hotel. "That's mine. The owners of this place are friends and let me keep it on the property."

He volunteered to take me to the local hot springs the next day. I agreed. That night, I stayed in his Airstream rather than my room. It was eccentrically decorated with collectibles from his travels across the Western and Southwestern United States: animal skulls, feathers, rocks, and crystals.

As I kissed him atop his Pendleton-covered bed, the one he had built with his own hands like everything else in the Airstream, I caught a whiff of the most offensive BO I'd ever encountered. The next morning, I let Joseph sleep and packed up my car for the drive home. I ran into some of the girls I had met at the oyster cookout and told them what happened. They started chuckling.

"Lee, you know Joseph is fifty-four, right?"

I knew he was older but had no idea he was that old. That was practically my dad's age. I had planned to ask the girls for their numbers in case they wanted to hang out the next time they were in LA, but now I was too embarrassed. I just quickly got in the car and drove off before Joseph saw me.

My sublet with Josie was only a month. I then moved to a shared three-bedroom in Echo Park. The other two girls were nice, but we didn't really connect. I hoped I'd make some friends at the healthy food conference Expo West, but all I came home with was four tote bags full of random samples like chickpea crackers and coconut meat jerky. Since I was no longer drinking, I thought maybe I could meet some sober people to be friends with. I found a recovery meeting in the small basement of a café in Silver Lake. The crowd was a dozen or so chain-smoking crust punks. In my Nike Day-Glo leggings and highlighter-yellow sneakers, I hardly fit in. This was even more clear as people went around the room telling stories of losing houses, cars, and marriages. Before I told my story, I acknowledged that I probably didn't belong there. But everyone dismissed this and encouraged me to continue. And afterward, a middle-aged woman with pink hair came up to me and introduced herself as Fiona.

"Here's my number," she said, taking a drag of her cigarette and exhaling. "You might need it someday." I did, but only because she was so polite.

One day, I received a DM from another influencer named Lucy. Lucy's IG page was a steady stream of yoga and plant-based recipes, but her focus was her own detox drink company.

Lucy had long auburn hair that cascaded perfectly over toned shoulders. She never wore a bra in her photos. I knew she was older than me from the kids that appeared in her posts. Had I not seen those, I would have suspected she was around my age. Her captions were always exuberant and excited. So was her DM.

> BABE!! Ur stuff is amazing! Let's meet up? Also, gotta give you a big box of my detox drinks!!!!

Given the community of like-minded women I'd met through the app back in New York, I quickly agreed. We met up at a smoothie place in West Hollywood. I got there first, ordered, and took a seat at a table. A few minutes later, Lucy walked in.

"BABE!" she yelled, as if we were old friends.

"Hi!" I said, surprised by her warmness. Lucy enveloped me in a hug. True to form, she was not wearing a bra, and I could see her nipples through her thin skinny-strap Free People tank. Then I noticed the man standing to her side.

"I brought my husband. I hope that's okay! We were dropping the kids off at school and just decided it was best if we both came."

Didn't she live in the Valley? How was this on the way?

The three of us sat down. Lucy did most of the talking. She was so upbeat and energetic, almost manic. Her husband just sat there quietly, staring at me. I felt a little unsettled and got up to leave as soon as I finished my smoothie. Lucy asked to trade numbers. Like with Fiona at the recovery group, I did so just to be polite, never expecting to talk to Lucy again.

But a few weeks later, overwhelmed by loneliness, I texted Lucy to see what she was doing. I figured maybe I'd been too judgmental. She responded instantly.

I'm packing for a trip I'm taking next week. Husband is out of town. Do you want to come here and sleep in bed with me? We can watch a movie, make a recipe, or smoke. Kids go to bed early.

I didn't know how to respond to that. I let thirty minutes pass, then texted: I think I'm just gonna do the same but at home. Have a great night!

A few weeks later, Lucy texted again. Babe. We're having a party tonight! Tory, Mira and June will be there!

Tory, Mira, and June were a Topanga-based yoga trio who were celebrities in the LA wellness world. Getting in with them could take my influencing to the next level.

Really? I texted.

Yes. You MUST come. The kids are at their grandparents. Mira has treats. We're going to do MDMA!

I hadn't done molly since moving to LA. But I was drowning in solitude and desperate to have some fun.

I arrived at Lucy's as dusk settled and, as she had instructed, went around to the back of the house. Milling around on the closely trimmed backyard grass were a half dozen women, none of them older than mid-thirties and all in yoga outfits, same as me. The only man present was Lucy's husband. Just like at the smoothie place, he said little and stared intently at us. I had barely finished introducing myself to each of the women and was about to strike up a conversation with one of the Topanga yogis when Lucy hollered.

"Okay! The moon is going to hit the equinox in ten minutes, so we better set our intentions!"

The backyard had been turned into what Lucy called a "cuddle puddle." She'd built a giant bed by placing couch cushions from the house's sofas and chairs beneath her children's teepee. Lucy pulled out a pack of American Spirits, unrolled one of the cigarettes, and sprinkled the tobacco onto the fake grass in some unexplained ceremony.

We then took a seat in the teepee and went around saying our intentions—mostly different versions of "I want to unblock my subconscious." Mine was "to let go of fear." But really, I just wanted to roll.

Mira handed out the rocks. I took four of them, letting the bitter synthetic melt on my tongue. Within minutes, I felt that familiar warmth flooding down my core, between my legs, and out to the ends of my fingers. A smile spread across my face and every move I made—stretching muscles, scratching skin, touching the Astroturf—felt like a mini orgasm. Mira's shit was really good.

Pretty soon, our hands found each other—interlocking fingers, caressing faces, rubbing shoulders, massaging scalps. The usual molly-induced sensation-seeking. Nothing sexual. At least not at first.

I made my way inside where there was another makeshift bed from pillows and couch cushions laid across the floor. This room also had a strobe light and Zedd playing from the speakers.

I then noticed Lucy's assistant—a young actress with long blonde hair, big tits, and blue eyes—climbing onto Lucy's husband's lap, her back arched, breasts pushed up toward his mouth.

Every time the lights hit the husband's face, I caught the lust in his eyes, locked onto the gift the assistant was offering him—her body.

I was shocked. I climbed outside on all fours to get Lucy, who was on her phone.

"I need him to come!" she said to me with a laugh.

"Who . . . come?" I asked, my words sounding like they were someone else's, so loud in my brain.

"Jared."

"Who . . . Jared?"

"My yoga teacher! I have *such* a crush on him. I want to *fuck* him, Lee!"

"Wait, but . . . is your husband okay with that?"

Lucy laughed so hard she toppled onto her side.

"Of course he is!"

I glanced back through the open doors at Lucy's husband. He was fondling the blonde assistant's breasts, her eyes closed and mouth open in ecstasy.

"Oh!" I said.

Then I fell back onto the pile of the other girls in the teepee. We were all twisted and tangled, groping and caressing.

I felt things sexually escalating, but I was so high I kept moving around, a growing sense of unease radiating from my core instead of ecstasy. I knew these girls from Instagram—what if this got out? Weren't we supposed to be pinnacles of health? But most of my anxiety came from knowing I'd sworn off drugs, and yet here I was, doing them again. I sat outside and stared at the stars, smoking the sacrificial American Spirits, only adding to my guilt.

I was rolling too hard to drive home, but around two a.m., my high wore off, and I felt the dark familiar cloud of a molly hangover come over me. I knew I was better than this, this drug-induced fake euphoria. I found a place on a sofa in the living room and forced myself to sleep for a few hours to the symphony of murmurs and moans happening across from me. At 5:45, I gathered my things, took a few sips of water from the sink, and got back into my car to drive home.

Thirteen

Though I didn't keep in touch with the Topanga yogis after that night, I started to integrate more yoga into my posts. Yoga was a part of the LA lifestyle. Instead of grabbing drinks like I would back East, now I met up with prospective friends for a vinyasa flow. Partying less meant I had more energy and an actual desire to take care of myself. To deepen my practice and learn more about its history, I enrolled in a thirty-day intensive yoga teacher training in Santa Monica. The day at the studio that I nailed a forearm stand, I rushed home and recorded myself doing it for a post.

My roommates were getting sick of me and the way I'd turned the apartment into my own private photo studio. One day I got a text on our group chat:

> hey Lee. Ur stuff is taking up a lot of room in the freezer. And your pantry items are spilling into our cabinets. When u get home tonight, can u clean up a bit?

I had to have so much food because I was still posting a smoothie bowl every single morning. Now, though, I was getting more creative with the background styling, including props like flowers and napkins that complemented the bowl's colors. One morning, I incorporated one of my roommates' favorite Pendleton blankets that was draped on the back of the couch. It rarely got cold enough to use it, so it was mostly decorative. Its colors and pattern perfectly showcased the smoothie. I laid the blanket on the floor, placed the smoothie on top of it, took a few photos, and posted the best one along with the recipe. As usual, the likes and comments quickly poured in.

Then I got a text from the roommate—directly, not on the group chat.

> Hey Lee. Is that my blanket in your latest IG post? I really don't appreciate that. You really need to ask me before using my things, especially something like that blanket. You put it on the floor and then put food on top of it? I feel disrespected.

I wanted a place of my own, but I couldn't yet afford it, even though the brand deals were steadily picking up. I got an email from a blender company who had seen my Instagram, Nutribullet, asking me to work for them full-time, developing recipes for them and testing out new equipment. I suggested a freelance structure instead, making a pitch to their CEO in the office that week, and they said yes. Urban Outfitters asked to photograph me for their new wellness section. A media company called Tastemade hired me to come to their Venice studio once a week to develop and prepare recipes around a specific theme, like Memorial Day BBQ potluck. They would supply the ingredients and I would make the meals on camera. And though they weren't paying me, a new brand called Outdoor Voices sent me a complete workout set of biker shorts, joggers, and a bra and asked me to post[6] it on their launch day with the hashtag #doingthings.

They were very selective about the people they sent this to. Most were niche celebrities. As a result of their strategic outreach, they quickly became a popular brand—especially their tri-colored leggings. Anytime they released a new product or colorway, they'd send me a new set. Soon I had over two dozen sets of Outdoor Voices leggings and crop tops. But I wasn't always able to easily fit in them. Usually by the end of the day, I would bloat so much that my clothes were almost unwearable, my stomach so distended I looked pregnant. I was constipated, gassy, and overwhelmingly tired. Around three p.m., my energy would plummet so intensely that I'd fall into a deep sleep through the afternoon and into the evening. I knew I was stressed about my financial situation and depressed from moving to a new city and knowing nobody, but this was a tiredness I'd never experienced before, and it was happening daily. I was also growing hairs on my chin rapidly.

These symptoms didn't jibe with my online persona—now my job. As a wellness influencer, I needed to look the picture of perfect health. I couldn't have hairs on my chin, spend days in bed, or sport a ring of fat around my belly that I couldn't lose.

I made an appointment with an endocrinologist. She took note of my symptoms, looked at my blood work, and said I had something called PCOS, or polycystic ovary syndrome. "Birth control can help alleviate some of the symptoms," she said. "But there's no cure."

I ran home and googled PCOS. What I read devastated me: *Infertility rates increase for those with PCOS. Obesity levels and hirsutism may also increase over the years.*

I found a book on Amazon about healing your PCOS naturally. I ordered it on my Kindle and read the entire thing in one night. The book was equal parts mystical and scientific. It talked about harnessing the power of your womanhood and aligning with your body instead of fighting against it. It also talked about the masculine way we live in our productivity-obsessed society, and how that could cause cortisol spikes. And it promoted a four-day cleanse to help rebalance your hormones.

The next morning, I went to the grocery store at six a.m. and bought all the ingredients for the cleanse. I started the day with soup and then had a salad for lunch. That night, my roommates and I drove to San Diego to see Father John Misty in concert. For Father John Misty, we could all put our differences aside.

My stomach was empty and making loud noises. I asked to turn the music up so my roommates wouldn't hear it. When we got to the venue, I was so hungry that my hands were shaking. I had three lemon seltzers, hoping to fill my belly, but it didn't work. By the time Father John Misty came on, I felt faint and could barely concentrate on the music.

I stayed silent in the back seat the whole way home, so hungry I was afraid if I spoke, I'd release a guttural scream. As soon as the car was parked, I ran up the stairs, opened a pack of rice cakes, and slathered some raw almond butter on top. My heart was racing like I had just come upon a gram of cocaine. I had one, two, then seven. I stood at the kitchen counter until I felt my hands stop shaking.

Before I went to bed, I posted a photo of a colorful dinnertime scene. I made no mention of PCOS or rice cakes.

Fourteen

I had met an industrial designer couple through Tate, and now they were asking if I could make granola for a pop-up event at their downtown loft. I hadn't made granola since moving to LA, and while they weren't offering payment, just covering the cost of ingredients, I saw an opportunity. They were well connected, and I figured it could lead to some further connections and opportunities with brands or other influential LA folks.

The loft was beautiful and very adult: Noguchi rice paper lamps, leather couches, abstract sculptures, even a dedicated tearoom in the mezzanine. The couple had a relationship with Stumptown Coffee, so Stumptown had dropped off a branded bicycle with an attached cooler cart filled with glass bottles of their cold brew.

I took note.

A local girl I'd seen around Echo Park, known for her sexy nature Instagram presence and her foraged, naturalist, sculptural bouquets, had provided the flowers for the event. She darted around the room like a fairy. She was always difficult to have a conversation with, which often surprised me. How could some people be so good at social media and have almost zero social skills IRL?

I wasn't sure what I was supposed to be doing. The granola was free for people to take, so it wasn't like I had to sell it to people and take their money. But it was clear I wasn't there as a guest. So I just stood there quietly beside my granola. I think my awkward energy weirded people out, because no one came to sample the granola. Until a man and a woman walked in carrying motorcycle helmets and wearing matching outfits of black jeans, black boots, and black leather jackets. The woman had a long jet-black bob and was around my height and age. She noticed the granola and headed right for it. She smiled at me with kind eyes and began scooping some out.

"Hi," I said nervously, unsure how I was supposed to be pitching my product. "That's my granola. I mean, you can have some, but I made it."

She took a bite.

"Wow! Is that chia in there?"

"Yeah!"

"Cinnamon too?"

"Uh-huh!"

Her name was Becca. She was very easy talk to, and we fell into a ten-minute conversation about which sceney restaurants were actually worth the wait (Dune in Atwater), who had the best avocados at the Wednesday Santa Monica farmer's market (JJ's Lone Daughter Ranch), and which wild fruit trees our streets had (hers had a loquat tree).

"I'm going up to Portland this weekend to go berry picking. Have you tried marionberries before?"

I shook my head.

"I'll bring some back for you. What's your number?"

I didn't get the same vibe from Becca as I had from Lucy, so I gave her my number without hesitation. But I didn't expect to hear from her—I'd lived in LA long enough to know that when people said "I'll definitely text you!" they rarely meant it.

But Becca did. The following Monday, I got a text from her asking when she could drop off my marionberries. She came over that night with a quart-sized Ball jar of them. They were a bit soggy from the plane ride but still delicious. We talked for almost three hours. She told me about growing up in the International House of Prayer church in Kansas City, which told its practitioners they were born evil and needed to purge themselves of their sins to expedite Jesus's return to rule the earth. She and her husband had moved to LA around the same time as me to get out of their cultish community and to start fresh and explore new grounds. When she left, we promised to hang out soon.

Now I had a real friend. And within the week, I got my first major brand partnership. The cereal brand Kashi had reached out and asked me to design and photograph a smoothie bowl for the back of their cereal box. They also asked me to do a few sponsored posts and travel up to a Squaw Valley resort to teach a smoothie bowl class at Wanderlust, a wellness festival happening later that year.

I asked Becca what she thought I should charge. Becca was working as a freelance photographer and urged me to ask Kashi about specifics like photo rights and usage laws. I made her an offer: Help me with the deal, read the contract, and she'd get to take a 10 percent cut of the brand partnership.

We put together a formal quote with line items detailing licensing fees, creative rights, social media posts, and my on-site events. I asked Kashi for $8,000.

They came back with $7,000.

I squealed with delight.

It was the most money I'd ever made from a single partnership. To me, it felt like $20,000.

A couple months later, I was browsing the cereal aisle at Whole Foods, and there it was: my smoothie bowl, enlarged to take up the entire back of a Kashi cereal box,[7] with my name and everything.

The moment was surreal. All around me, people were shopping

hurriedly. It was just another day for them, but deep inside I felt powerful and strong. If I could do this, what else could I do?

I bought the box, then called my parents and told them to head to their local Stop & Shop to pick up a box for themselves.

That night, Becca came over, and we took photos of me holding up the box in my apartment. I was so pleased with myself. I didn't know how to fully wrap my head around what was happening.

Working with a well-known food brand like Kashi made me less intimidated to get dinner with the staff of *Bon Appétit* magazine at the Chateau Marmont. I was invited by a chef influencer named Thomas. He lived in New York, and we'd been exchanging DMs for the last couple months. He was in town working on a video series for the magazine. It was easy to see why they wanted him on camera. He was cute—tall and muscular with straight blonde hair.

That afternoon, he'd come to my apartment to help me make a smoothie bowl. I often did collaborations with other bloggers, chefs, foodies, and more. It was a way to combine audiences and connect communities. Plus, followers loved when they saw two of their favorite personalities collaborate. We were flirting hard as we made the bowl, took photos, and talked about what the captions should say. But the excitement I felt by the sexual tension was instantly intensified by the prospect of hanging out with the Bon App team. They had recently brought on a wave of young creatives and were making a name for themselves as a trendy, food-centric brand. I thought it would be a good opportunity to show my face while also seeing where things went with Thomas.

Too cheap for valet, I parked on the street, walked into the hotel restaurant, and found Thomas and a group of fifteen other Bon App staff seated at a long banquet table. I had decided that I would have a drink or two, just so that it wasn't a whole thing of me not drinking and having to explain why to people.

I told Thomas I'd have whatever he was having. He ordered me a Don Julio on the rocks with soda water and lime. He'd already had a few and was pretty hammered. I was trying to make conversation with the other people, but he kept interrupting and being loud and obnoxious. I could tell he was annoying people, and I worried that they would be annoyed with me by association. I figured the best way to make a good impression with them would be to lead Thomas away from the group.

Shortly after finishing my drink, I led him from the table, and we went up to his courtyard-facing room. Not having drunk in a while, I was pretty buzzed and horny. We hurriedly undressed each other and fucked quickly as murmurs of conversation and faint music floated up from the courtyard. When Thomas finished, he rolled off me, beads of sweat on his forehead.

"I can't believe I just had sex with Lee From America, the smoothie bowl girl," he said.

My immediate reaction was pride, but that quickly dissolved into disgust. I was just a conquest for him. I was sure he'd have no discretion and brag about it to his friends back in New York. He wasn't interested in me. He was interested in the online version of me. At this point, I was still aware that those were two separate things.

I put my underwear back on, got dressed, grabbed my mother's vintage Levi's jean jacket, and left Thomas naked and passed out on the bed. I didn't even consider going back to the dinner. I went straight to my car and drove home in silence.

Fifteen

One morning when I opened Instagram, I found a message alerting me to a new feed—what was being called "the algorithm." No longer were posts shown chronologically. Now there was a mysterious series of systems at work that tailored your feed based off data.

Likes on my posts quickly went from an average of twelve hundred to eight hundred. It was harder to get my posts noticed. Everyone was panicking. Influencers were begging their followers to turn on their notifications so that they'd get notified of posts and would be sure not to miss them. I found this cringe and decided to take a different approach. I thought to myself, *If my content is good, it will get noticed.*

I started posting with even more frequency—at least three times a day, every day.

I also started posting more pictures of myself. I noticed photos with me in them would get more likes than my food posts. People wanted to see me.

And I began experimenting with various topics to see what performed better on the algorithm: posts about mental health, bad-body image days, eating disorder recovery. The day after Donald

Trump was elected, I posted a picture[8] of myself doing a full wheel pose wearing a gifted outfit from Free People. The caption said:

> today was heavy. i took the morning off from social media because my brain and heart needed to. ask what you can do for your community, today, right now, to make the world a better place. for me, that meant a little social media detox and heading to a campsite with a friend to sleep under the stars to collect my thoughts ✧ lets not be discouraged, but channel this energy to INSPIRE. my heart is with you america

I wasn't particularly political, but everyone else was posting about it, so I thought I should too. When women marched on Washington wearing pink pussy hats, I posted multiple emojis with different shades of skin exhibiting my openness to diversity. I thought I understood what it meant and I felt empowered for posting it, but there was also a pressure to. Everybody else was. If I didn't, I feared the omission might be recognized by my followers and turn them off.

One day I posted about my recent decision to move away from veganism and start eating eggs. I was afraid of coming out as non-vegan, thinking that the vegan community would shame me. But I had a feeling that authenticity and confidence would beat out the noise, and it paid off. The comments were flooded with people thanking me, saying they had stopped being vegan too but had been afraid to admit it for the same reason I was.

I'd beaten the algorithm and made my way through to people's feeds again.

Some influencers turned their comments off, but I always kept mine on. What set me apart from most wellness influencers was how normal and approachable I was. I felt turning off the comments would suggest I thought I was better than my followers. If anything, my followers were better than me. They were supportive, kind, and encouraging. As with any social media platform, those initial days were all about positivity and community. I sincerely loved hearing from people. I loved knowing that I wasn't alone in my insecurities and worries. It gave me a sense of connection that, aside from my new friend Becca, I had struggled to find in LA.

This connection was further solidified when I received an email from Poketo, a brand and shop known for its stylish workshops, inviting me to teach a workshop around health and wellness. I put together an event that included a recipe demonstration of my layered carrot-cake oats, a DIY breakfast bar, a talk on healthy eating, and a forty-minute yoga workout with a local instructor I'd met on IG. The session sold out so fast we instantly set up another workshop for the next day. This also sold out. After the two-hour sessions, many of the attendees came up to me afterward, expressing their gratitude and excitement. I split the revenue from the event with Poketo fifty-fifty.

Back in my apartment that evening, I sat by the window, sipping a cup of tea and looking out at the twinkling city lights. I thought back to a year and a half ago, when my mom drove me to the airport for my flight to LA.

"How are you going to support yourself if this doesn't work out?" she asked.

"Mom, I'll figure it out," I said.

She kept her eyes on the road and didn't respond. I knew she didn't believe that I could be successful. I thought about calling her to tell her about the workshops. It was late back East, but she was probably still up. I picked up my phone and instead opened Instagram.

Sixteen

From my eggs post, I saw a 500 percent spike in likes, comments, and views.

My following hit sixty thousand.

Then Instagram tweaked the app again.

One morning, I opened it to find the interface looked different. At the top was a row of icons of people I followed. I clicked the first icon, another health food blogger in LA. Suddenly, a video filled my screen.

"Hey, guys!" she said brightly. She was in her spotless living room, not a pillow out of place. Her appearance was just as perfect: soft straight blonde hair pulled back into a pony, bright blue eyes twinkling, face unblemished, even tan, diamonds encrusting her ears.

"I'm trying out Instagram Stories for the first time," she said. "It's cool, right?"

A wave of panic washed over me—and not just because I felt so inferior to this exquisite human specimen. I was having a hard enough time keeping up with my new volume of posting since the algorithm was introduced. Now I was going to have to post even more.

Soon I was posting five or six stories throughout the day to complement my grid posts.

The good thing about stories was that it allowed you to post content that was a lot more casual. Since the posts would disappear after twenty-four hours—clearly, this feature had been introduced as a response to the growing popularity of Snapchat—it didn't need to be so heavily thought out. I'd take my followers with me on my morning workouts—whether it be yoga, the gym, or a hike at Griffith Park. Then, in addition to a grid post of my intricate breakfast every morning, I also started uploading a daily story of my morning caffeinated beverage: a hot, bright, creamy matcha "latte" prepared in the latest Vitamix the brand had just gifted me, made with hot water, coconut butter, cinnamon, and a dozen or so various adaptogens and powders including collagen, ashwagandha, and reishi. I'd pour the piping-hot drink into one of my artisan stoneware mugs—each a unique variation made by a local female ceramicist—adding to the earthy vibes, balanced by an upbeat tempo song playing from my speaker (back before stories let you add an actual song). I loved introducing my followers to new music like Electric Guest, Rubblebucket, Parcels, and Toro y Moi. Around this time, I became known online as "the matcha girl."

Though the aim was to create a breezy, incidental vibe, my morning matcha stories were curated down to the last detail, including the perky windowsill succulents in the background, which added the perfect touch of natural-girl charm.

My views racked up, but the popularity began to erode my relaxed approach to stories. I felt the expectation to post my morning routine every day, as that's what my followers expected. If I took a day off, the algorithm might punish me and I'd be pushed off people's feeds. I made a strategic business decision and moved into a one-bedroom apartment in an Art Deco building in Koreatown. I could barely afford it, but it had a newly renovated kitchen and six windows that let in incredible light, and I figured the setting would be a way to build my audience and hopefully bring in more business. In the stories that I was now calling "Matcha Mornings," I stood in the pristine kitchen with the early-morning Los Angeles sun streaming in and poured the bright green foam into a mug with muted pinks, mauve, and terracotta triangles to echo a California sunset.

My stories performed astronomically well, consistently getting around one hundred thousand views. This caught the attention of William Morris Endeavor, or WME, one of the world's largest talent agencies. They represented some of the most famous entertainers in the world: models, actors, musicians, athletes. Now, apparently, they were looking to represent influencers. They emailed me asking to set up a meeting in their New York office.

I was more nervous than excited. I'd interviewed with a talent agency once, and it did not go well.

When I was twelve, I took a predawn train into Manhattan with my mother, sister, aunt, and cousins to watch the *Today* show live from Rockefeller Center Plaza. They were hosting a live performance from the cast of the new Broadway revival of *Oklahoma!* My family loved musicals, but Broadway tickets were so expensive that we were always looking for a deal. This was our opportunity to experience the show for free. We dressed in Western costumes: cowboy hats and boots, bandannas, and denim jackets.

It now occurs to me it was the first time I'd manipulated my identity on-screen to win the approval of others. As Al Roker and the camera operator strolled the perimeter of the metal barricade, deciding which lucky tourists they would select to interview, my family in unison pointed at me and yelled, "It's her birthday!" It was not my birthday. But the night before, as we decorated our cardboard signs, the group decided this strategy gave us the best chance of getting on TV. My sign read: I MAY NOT BE FROM OKLAHOMA BUT TODAY IS MY BIRTHDAY!

"It's okay, it's just a little white lie," my mom said.

It worked. Al and the camera operator stopped in front of us. The camera's light was switched on. It was like a beam from heaven—so bright I had to shield my eyes for a moment.

"You ready to be on TV?" Al asked.

"Yeah!" my family screamed. I joined them but less emphatically. That camera light felt like the light they shine on someone in a police interrogation room in the movies. I felt so guilty. I worried America's most beloved weatherman was somehow going to realize he was being duped and shame me on national television. Fortunately, he simply wished me a happy birthday, I muttered a thank-you, Al and the camera operator walked on, and my family and I all high-fived.

Afterward, we had some time before our train home, so we walked up to Bloomingdale's to window-shop. I went up the escalator to the contemporary women's section and beelined for the Juicy Couture racks, flipping through their latest collection of terry cloth tracksuits. Most of the kids in my school were wearing Juicy and other high-end brands like Michael Starr and 7 for All Mankind. I couldn't afford these—unless I found seasons-old versions discounted at Loehmann's. So I relished getting to fondle the lush material and imagine what it would be like to have a closet full of it like my classmates. After a couple minutes, a smooth, faintly European voice pulled me out of my daydreaming.

"Darling, hi. Where's your mother?"

This woman was naturally tall, and even more so in her four-inch heels. She had a Bluetooth headset in her ear—well before that became common—that she lightly tapped with a nude-manicured nail. Her black hair was gathered behind her head in a sleek pony, not a follicle out of place.

I pointed to my mom on the other side of the floor. It was easy to spot her in her cowboy hat. I trailed behind the woman as she glided over to my mom, said something I couldn't overhear, handed her a card, then clacked away down the white tiles out of sight.

"Mom, what did she want?"

My mom raised her eyebrows, smiling and shocked, and handed me the card:

ELITE MODELING AGENCY

"That lady wondered if you'd ever thought about modeling. She's asked us to schedule an appointment to come back into the city and see her."

My friend Maggie had done some modeling and once got to miss a few days of school in the middle of February for a Ralph Lauren photo shoot in Turks and Caicos, where she stayed in a thatched-roof hut on the beach with her parents. She had that all-American look, with olive-kissed skin and a Cindy Crawford–style beauty mark above her pouty pink lips. I was jealous she got to keep her lime-green and watermelon-pink polo shirts after the shoot. Modeling made sense for her but not for me. I was pale with freckles and wore braces—the metal brackets and wires fixed to my teeth to correct my overbite. That month, I'd chosen baby-blue rubber bands. I wondered what this woman saw in me.

A few weeks later, my mother and I showed up for our appointment at the twenty-fourth floor of a midtown skyscraper. The view was breathtaking—wall-to-wall windows revealed the city sprawled below, the trees of Madison Square Park resembling broccoli. Just as stunning were the women who worked in the office. If these were just the employees, how beautiful did you have to be to be one of their models? I sat in the lobby drinking my complimentary bottle of Evian and flipping through one of the agency's portfolios, the plastic sheets holding photographs of various sharp-boned women staring unenthusiastically back at me. I had spent the night before stressing about what to wear, debating with my mom for hours, settling on an Abercrombie & Fitch tee with the word HEARTBREAKER (my choice) and low-rise khaki pants from Old Navy (her choice). I was excited about my outfit, but looking at those photos I realized it didn't matter what I wore. How could I ever compare with these girls? Again, I wondered why that woman had stopped me in Bloomingdale's.

I guess she wondered the same thing, because once we were escorted back to her office, we only remained for a few minutes. Her name was Winona. She had been a model herself and was now an executive scout. From behind her big desk, she asked how tall I was—and also the heights of my mom, my dad, and their parents. The shortest was five feet four inches, the tallest six feet. This did not seem to impress Winona.

"Here's the thing," she said, taking off her reading glasses with a sigh. "This industry is tough, and I mean tough. It's not great for young girls' self-esteem. Lee would need to leave school, and even then, it's not guaranteed she would make it. Also, your family's height lineage is . . ."

She trailed off without finishing the sentence, then began fiddling with a stack of papers. It was clear the meeting was over. I wondered why she had us come all the way into the city when she could have asked the questions about our heights over the phone and spared us the time and embarrassment—especially if she was so concerned with young girls' self-esteem.

With this experience in mind, I didn't get my hopes up about my meeting with WME, but I knew I'd be okay without them too. I didn't put too much thought into what I wore—a Gap denim jacket over an organic slub cotton tee with a gifted Madewell red bandanna tied around my neck and wide-leg Free People sailor pants on the bottom. But the outcome was different this time. In a sleek conference room in their big fancy office in midtown Manhattan, a team of six people in dark business casual sat around a table pitching me hard on why I should let them represent me. I signed a contract, and they wasted no time getting to work. When I woke up in my hotel room the next day, my Instagram account was verified.

Seventeen

Now that I was with WME, they started negotiating higher rates for my incoming partnership inquiries. I was sent on my first influencer trip to an olive oil farm in Northern California, joined by three other influencers. I wouldn't be paid, but I viewed it as a free trip. We stayed in a shabby-chic hotel outside Sacramento. My room had a rustic antique mirror in which I took a few hundred selfies. We ate dinner under strings of Edison bulbs and to the accompaniment of a live bluegrass band. The main event was a guided tour of the farm. The four of us didn't have much to say to each other—we'd exhausted our small talk over dinner—but when we piled into the olive truck's cherry picker and recorded ourselves, we made sure to smile for the camera and throw our arms around each other as if we were best friends.

Nike flew me to New York City to post about their Apple Watch collaboration. Again, I wasn't paid, but the trip and expenses were free. At the Nike store in SoHo, I was given an Apple Watch and an assortment of leggings, bras, jackets, and sneakers to take home. I changed into the clothes, strapped on the watch, and jogged around the city with three world-class runners, posting the experience as I went.

UGG hired me to star in one of their video series, create a

sponsored post, and cook a dinner for other celebrity influencers they hosted in the Hollywood Hills. The writer and comedian Mindy Kaling also hired me to cook lunch for her all week. This was surreal, but not much different than a private chef job.

One morning, I arrived at a Venice bungalow at nine o'clock with my Vitamix and grocery bags full of my favorite breakfast items. I'd been hired by Joey, the husband of one of my followers. Every year, he took his wife on a birthday trip, usually somewhere exotic, but this time, they were headed to Catalina Island. To make it extra special, he paid me, her favorite influencer, to surprise her with a homemade breakfast and an in-house visit before their boat ride.

"She's such a fan," he whispered as I entered the house. "It's so awesome you're here."

While his wife continued to sleep, I quietly set up my workstation. Then, Joey went to wake her up. She came padding down the stairs in slippers and a robe, her hair disheveled. I stood, smiling at the kitchen island, trying to make it seem like all of this was natural.

At first, Nina looked at me confused, a stranger in her kitchen, her sleep-fogged brain unable to catch up. Then it dawned on her.

"No way," she said. Then she shrieked: "NO WAY!"

"Yep, that's Lee From America!" Joey said.

I waved, feeling awkward and detached.

"SHUT THE FUCK UP!" she yelled, then jumped into Joey's arms.

"She's here to cook breakfast with you, babe! You get her till eleven."

Nina was shaking. "I need to change. Okay. Oh my God. Okay. I'll be right back down!"

Joey looked at me and smiled.

"This is so crazy!" he said.

Nina came back downstairs in jean shorts and a band tee. The shaking didn't stop. Even her voice was shaking.

"I'm still in shock," she said. "I've been following you for years. Can I get a selfie with you?"

She still hadn't grasped that her husband had paid me to be there and she could have as many selfies as she wanted. With the kitchen's pendant lights casting an unflattering yellow sheen over everything, I smiled as we pressed our heads close together and she took a photo. Then she immediately opened Instagram and posted it.

"Do you do this a lot, Lee?" asked Nina, not looking up from her phone, watching to see the likes come in.

"Can't say I do," I said. "This is definitely a first."

I was so busy that I decided to hire an assistant. I wrote a job description on Instagram Stories and received around three hundred emails and résumés, mostly from young girls who clearly were more interested in becoming influencers themselves than assisting me. The person I hired worked fifteen hours per week, helping with scheduling and other admin like booking travel for the workshops I was starting to do more of. I flew to Chicago to host two back-to-back workshops called Matcha Mornings. There were about fifty people per workshop, and they sold out within an hour.

My body became run down from the uptick in work and travel, and I was always trying to adjust and lock in my diet. I went from lightly moving away from veganism with just eggs to eating mostly meat and vegetables. Then I started a twenty-one-day smoothie cleanse. Toward the end of that, I fell sick with the flu. But I couldn't let that stop me from posting. With a 103-degree fever, I crawled out of bed, cleaned up the mountain of tissues and honey cough drop wrappers, and changed from my sweat-soaked pajamas into a Spiritual Gangster tank that said NAMASTE and one of my dozens of pairs of gifted Outdoor Voices joggers. I put on fake glasses from Garrett Leight that I'd been gifted and opened my laptop, even though I was too sick to look at the screen. I held a smoothie, even though I was too sick to eat it.[9]

Eighteen

I began a partnership with a functional medicine clinic to further find the perfect diet for my body. In exchange for posting about them a few times a year, I got to meet with a functional nutritionist. I wanted to get my period back. I didn't want to be bloated or gassy anymore. I wanted my body to be back in my control.

We experimented with cutting out avocado, cauliflower, and peanuts. Then one afternoon after peeing, I noticed blood on the toilet paper. My period had arrived. It had been three months since my last one.

I decided to be honest on Instagram with my period story: how it had vanished with my disordered eating in high school, how it had remained irregular ever since, how I'd been diagnosed with PCOS, how doctors encouraged me to take hormones but I instead pursued more holistic treatments.

The likes and comments poured in—the most comments I'd ever gotten on a personal post.

Thanks for sharing girl! You are def not alone.

The struggle with PCOS is real—thanks for sharing!

Say it girl!

Needed to hear this girl!

My DMs stayed lit all night long. I realized I had unlocked an entire content strategy. The more personal, the better. The more extreme, the better. I started going hard on "I quit" posts: why I quit coffee, why I quit caffeine, why I quit sugar. These posts performed so well, and the algorithm seemed to favor them. My account was featured a few times on the app's Explore page, which seriously boosted my follower count. Each post was garnering an average of ten thousand likes and more than one hundred comments. I started to be recognized in public. One day at Echo Park Lake, someone screamed: "LEEEEE!"

I turned and saw it was Chloe Fineman, a comedian popular on Instagram who would later go on to be a *Saturday Night Live* cast member.

"I'm such a huge fan," she shouted. "LOVE YOUR STUFF!"

I was growing about seven thousand followers per month and quickly approaching one hundred thousand.

It was important for influencers to do big announcement posts anytime they hit a big milestone. I decided to create the shape of "100" made entirely from a viral recipe I'd created named "fat balls." Made from coconut shreds, coconut butter, and various nuts and seeds, these were a high-fat, low-sugar alternative to the more fruit-and-date heavy "bliss balls" that had been part of the vegan 80/10/10 diet trend years earlier. Culture was finally open to eating healthy fats after the low-fat trends of the earlier 2000s.

I got to rolling my fat balls. I bought confetti. I drafted the caption, aiming for just the right amount of humblebrag.

#leefromamerica has transformed from simply a recipe sharing platform to a place where I can be 100% honest with my experiences, health journey, and other parts of my life with you guys. i feel so humbled to be able to use my voice and writing in this way.

Going to bed that night, I had 99,989 followers. When I woke up the next morning, the milestone achieved, I posted[10] my fat balls celebration and got 280 messages of congratulations. I was elated for a few hours. Then I set my sights on two hundred thousand.

Nineteen

I was spending at least ten hours per day on Instagram. My Instagram routine was the same nearly every morning. I'd upload a story of me on my way to my morning workout (usually SoulCycle or an Equinox class; both memberships were gifted), then my Matcha Mornings pouring video, then a grid post midmorning of either my matcha or an intricate breakfast. Then I would do a series of story posts in the late morning, normally seven to eight videos that were fifteen seconds each. In these, I'd host a Q&A or pose reflective questions for women—like why we're always the ones to apologize when someone bumps into us—or share step-by-step tutorials, such as how I organized my fridge. Then I would do another grid post in the early afternoon about a topic like dry brushing, oil training, fasting, or PCOS, followed by two to three more stories. Then I might do a third and final grid post at night: my dinner, a photo of my candlelit tub, an evening adaptogenic tea blend, or some before-bed stretching. Each grid post took hours to style and shoot. Then I had to select the photo from the dozens—sometimes more than a hundred—I had taken. Then I edited and retouched it—making myself brighter, my clothes pop, the greenery or sky pop too. I also photoshopped out any wires, electrical outlets, or other nonorganic things from my pictures. I used the Snapseed photo app for brightening specific areas, and then VSCO's K3 filter for an overall sunny glow. After posting, I'd sit hunched over my phone as the comments poured in. I could tell within the first minute if the post would do well; I'd studied and memorized my post analytics. If it got seventy-three likes within a minute of going up, it would be "successful" in my eyes.

I responded to every comment, even with just an emoji. It made the overall comment number look like it was higher. It also drove engagement. Commenters loved to be acknowledged. I knew this from my own experience commenting on posts by Loni Jane.

More and more, I felt in competition with other influencers on Instagram. If I decided to have a little extra time to myself and didn't open the app until nine a.m., I would see another wellness influencer who'd already uploaded breakfast and eight stories of what she was doing with her morning: a five a.m. workout class, back home to take care of the kids, a smoothie, a bulletproof coffee, playing with her kids. The more people storied and posted, the more I felt I needed to too.

If a photo went up and didn't get many likes, I would be crushed. Part of it was insecurity and the need to feel validated, but it was also about business. Whenever brands offered money for a post, I'd have to send them my statistics. And a photo with low likes brought down your monthly averages and impacted a brand's willingness to hire you.

Before I signed with WME, Becca and I had taken quick camping trips outside the city every few weeks. We loved to sit under the stars together, drink tea, and make "camping tacos" of cubed sweet potato, onions, and black beans that we'd sauté in a cast-iron pan over the fire. However, now that I had full-time representation and was devoting even more of my time to influencing, we started hanging out less—from three times a week to once or twice a month. So Becca and

I took a quick overnight trip to the Angeles National Forest to reconnect. But even then, I was still working on the car ride home, silently responding to emails when we'd normally be chatting.

That was the case anytime I'd hang out with the few friends I had. One night a couple girlfriends and I went to dinner at a fancy restaurant in Malibu. I wore a backless sundress with spaghetti straps and kitten heels I got secondhand on Poshmark. I didn't usually wear heels; it wasn't part of my brand. But I had to do a sponsored post for the insurance company Blue Shield, and heels seemed on brand for them. The theme of the post was balancing a healthy lifestyle while also having a social life.

I continued to let my followers in on all the "shameful" parts of my history. I was often making jokes about how I used to be at the club until four a.m. and now I was waking up around that time to meditate and work out—or how I used to pregame after dinner and now I was sudsing in a bathtub full of rose petals and essential oils. I was in full self-care mode—even wearing a gold cursive necklace that said HOMEBODY. I was proud of the shift: going from coked-out nights to taking really good care of myself. I was still rarely drinking, and all this self-care tied into work meant spending more time alone at home, not hanging out with friends. Being social still felt synonymous with gathering around drinks or staying up late—both of which would throw off my routine and my brand.

So, since I was going to be out socializing with friends amid the picturesque setting of Malibu, I figured it made sense to take the photo that night.

We were a little early for our dinner reservation, so we took a stroll along the pier. My friends chatted casually about their latest boy troubles, and I chimed in with the occasional "hah!" But I was more focused on scanning our surroundings for the best photo backdrop and watching the sunset, waiting for the moment when the light was perfect.

I settled on my spot: the pier's sun-washed wood in the foreground and the foamy ocean in the background. The sky looked magical as it changed from pink to blue.

I held my phone out to my friends.

"Do you guys mind taking a picture of me?" I asked.

To get the photo and angle I wanted, I found it worked best to first take a photo of whoever was taking my picture so they could see the exact framing I had in mind. I'd ask a friend to pose in my spot, take her picture, then have her return to the camera position to photograph me.

"Okay," I instructed, "so you are going to stand here, holding the phone here. Hold the phone exactly here. I'm going to stand there."

"Wow," my friend said, looking at the picture I took of her. "That's a good photo."

"I know," I said. "I know all the angles."

I got into my spot and began posing for the camera, but I felt uptight and nervous. There were other people walking along the pier, watching me. So much depended on this. Blue Shield was expecting first-round edits on Monday. It had to be good.

My friend took twenty pictures. I could tell because my sound was on, and my iPhone made the fake shutter-clicking sound.

"Okay!" she said, lowering the phone.

I knew it wasn't enough. I knew I wouldn't be satisfied. I was no longer smiling.

"Can you take a few more?" I asked.

"Yep!" my friend said.

My smile came back on with the clack of the camera. I pulled out my classic poses: keeping my arms out at my sides and rotating in a slight twirl, casually walking toward the camera, alternating smiling with my teeth and with my mouth closed. My friend periodically put the phone down, suggesting that she was done. I continued posing, making it clear she was not.

After at least one hundred clicks, I stopped posing and walked over to see how the pictures looked. I didn't like any of them. She hadn't taken my directions. She was holding the phone too high—too "top-down." My head was huge and my body too small. Eye level or below was much better. It looked more authentic.

"Ugh," I said. "I'm so sorry, but can you take a few more?"

My friends looked at me with both annoyance and concern.

"We're going to be late for our reservation," one of them said.

"It'll be quick," I said. "I promise."

An awkward silence penetrated the air.

"Sure," said my friend with the camera, which she raised back into position.

I stepped back into place. There were only a couple more minutes of great light, so I was more assertive in directing my friend. "Keep the camera angle straight on . . . a bit lower . . . no, not that low."

My friend adjusted as I smiled, trying out a variety of expressions like a fake cackling laugh. I felt some shame for annoying my friends and for the self-indulgent nature of my job. I did my best to ignore the passersby looking on, but I felt judged, and I was judging myself.

This may not look like a job to others, but this is your job, Lee. A few minutes of work now can mean tons of validation and money in the bank later. This was the mantra I reminded myself of anytime I felt self-conscious taking photos in public.

I took a deep breath and did my best to focus. Getting the right photo[11] mattered way more than what anyone, including my friends, thought. In the caption, I noted how important it was to surround yourself with understanding and loving people.

Becca was the friend I felt I could totally unplug with. No editing, no performance, no photographs, just presence. For months, she and I had been planning a four-day hiking trip in Yosemite. It would be my first visit, but Becca had been there several times. She rhapsodized about the wide-open spaces, the colors, and the quiet. "It's the most beautiful and peaceful place you'll ever see," she said. But as the trip approached, I was growing increasingly anxious. There was limited cell service where we'd be camping. That had also been the case on our Angeles National Forest trip, and at the time I'd relished having a slight reprieve from social media. But now I worried that if I didn't post for a few days, I would be causing irrevocable damage to my career.

Becca texted me the day before we were supposed to leave.

> I'll bring all the gear. Can you take care of breakfast and dinner our first two days, and I'll handle the last two days? I'm thinking camping tacos and buckwheat pancakes!!! I'm getting so excited!

I didn't respond. I couldn't think about campfire tacos. I had to post a recipe for cinnamon-spiced sweet potatoes and photograph an almond butter drizzle smoothie.

That night, Becca texted me again.

> What time will you come scoop me?

I let the text linger, willing it to go away.

An hour later: ?

The anxiety was growing so intense now. I couldn't leave my phone for one day, let alone four. My followers might forget about me. My hot streak with the algorithm might turn cold. I wasn't willing to risk it. I'd worked too hard to get to this point.

Around nine p.m.: Lee?

Finally, I picked up the phone and called her. I had no idea what I was going to say.

"Hi," she said with trepidation in her voice.

"I'm so sorry," I said, "but I just don't think I can swing this trip."

Silence filled the line.

"I hope you understand, it's just, my job right now—"

"Okay," she said. "My feelings are definitely hurt."

I felt horrible knowing I'd disappointed someone that I loved—knowing I was more concerned about my followers than my best friend. I lay on the floor with my body curled into a ball.

"I just can't leave work right now. It's too crazy with everything. I just can't afford to be offline."

"Okay," Becca said hollowly.

She sent a text right after we hung up: I can't believe you waited until the night before we were supposed to leave for an eight-hour road trip. I'd packed the car and everything. I'm pretty wrecked. I don't know what to do.

I apologized again. I knew this likely meant the end of our friendship. Awful as I felt, I still made sure to do my last post of the day.

Twenty

While I admitted to myself that I should have handled the situation with Becca better, I was not ready to admit that my online life might be dangerously rewiring my brain and causing harmful damage to my real life. Instead, I absolved myself of any blame by telling myself that this was just the nature of the job, that sometimes friendships end. I was just on a different path than my friends. They simply didn't understand the new direction my career was taking me in. Maybe they were even a little jealous. They were holding me back. They were the problem, not me—and definitely not social media. The answer was not to do any further self-examination but to find new friends in the influencing community who would better understand my ambition and the demands of my job.

One of these was a woman named Brooke, who had DM'd me asking if I'd like a complimentary session of breathwork healing. She was a single mother who lived in Venice and had the de rigueur petiteness and flowing blonde hair of an influencer. She didn't have a huge following, but her bio said "Reiki certified," and I was always curious to try new wellness trends. This was my first time hearing about breathwork.

She came to my apartment and kneeled over me as I lay on my living room floor—in nearly the same spot as where I'd spent my phone call with Becca.

"I work with females to help uplevel their business, clear their consciousness, and step into their highest self," Brooke said. "I was drawn to you, Lee, because you're a magnetic presence. All these people are drawn to you. What are you doing to help yourself?"

Brooke then lit some sage and played some shamanic drumming on the wireless speaker she'd brought with her. She instructed me to exhale and inhale. Periodically, she would hold on to my ankle, or place a crystal on my heart, or massage my head. I found myself slipping in and out of consciousness, listening to Brooke's coaching and the music. It felt great. Soon, it was over, and I opened my eyes.

"Wow, that was powerful," Brooke said. "Your lips were blue, which is a good sign. It means something inside you died. I saw your inner child. I saw a lot of your ancestors. How do you feel?"

"Incredible," I said. "Toward the end, I couldn't move any of my body parts. My legs felt numb, but they were somehow still buzzing."

"That sounds about right!" Brooke said.

I told her how quickly my business was growing, how much I was working, how stressful the job was.

"You're on the precipice of something great, Lee," she said. "I'd love to help you get there."

She would regularly send me DMs like: Tonight, stand at the window and gaze up at the moon with your feet firmly planted on the ground.

When I mentioned using a period cup rather than tampons, she instructed me to save the blood and use it as a face mask. It's full of stem cells! she said.

Curious, the next time I was on my period, I took the cup out, dipped my finger into the warm, dark blood, and put two streaks under my eyes like a football player. I was so disgusted that I never tried this again. However, I did take another follower's advice and regularly mixed my period blood with two quarts of water to water my plants.

Every time I shared a new wellness hack on Instagram, it seemed like the next discovery was already waiting to be revealed. There was an endless amount of alternative remedies and solutions that I was constantly learning about. This also meant endless content to create.

One day, I posted a series of stories where I threw away all my mainstream household cleaners and replaced them with nontoxic substitutes, citing the harmful effects of artificial fragrances and harsh chemicals.

And every time I did a sponsored post or big project, Brooke would reply to my stories: Yes girl! Upleveling!

I also made friends on the influencer work trips I was more regularly taking. A group of us—all with followings of at least one hundred thousand—were flown to Austin to visit and post about a tortilla chip brand on Cinco de Mayo. I wasn't paid, but they put us up in an eleven-bedroom, five-bathroom mansion in the heart of the city. There was some petty high school drama about who would get the biggest room. It got so heated that by the end of the trip, many of the girls weren't talking to each other. But in the photos,[12] we all look happy and chummy. That was the unspoken nature of our job, after all: to always look like we were having a great time.

Lululemon flew me and a few other influencers first-class to Maui. This job also didn't pay, but I was happy to collaborate with one of my favorite brands. A black van picked us up from the airport and drove us high up into the island's forests to a secluded five-star resort. First we were ushered into a room filled with new Lululemon clothes and told we could pick whatever we wanted. Then we were shown to our lodgings: each of us had an entire villa situated among the beautiful green hills.

It quickly became clear that I wouldn't be developing lasting friendships with these influencers. They spent most of the trip trying to find mushrooms and acid. The only one I connected with was a lovely man named Pat who was a yoga influencer from the Pacific Northwest.

"Lee, you're growing so fast," he said. "You are collecting those emails? Instagram will probably go away one day. Those emails will last forever."

One of the stories I posted showed off my new Lululemon joggers. I saw that a man named Evert was one of the first people to view it. I'd hoped he would be. The first time he DM'd me was a few weeks before.

You are very pretty 🖤

I clicked through to his profile. There were less than twenty pictures uploaded. Photos of two young girls, bright blonde with big blue eyes. Photos from airplane windows. A photo of him in a brown suit, perfectly fitted to his body, holding up the two girls—who I assumed were his daughters. The sun shined on all three of them. He was beautiful.

Holy fuck, I thought. *Is he real?*

I looked closer at the photos. They were all geolocated in a language I didn't recognize. It seemed he lived in Sweden.

Thanks! I responded.

I'm in LA, Evert wrote. Where can I get a good breakfast bowl?

Honey Hi or Café Gratitude, I wrote.

Thanks!

I closed our chat and kept storying. A few hours later, I got another message from Evert: a photo of his breakfast bowl.

It was very good. Thank u for the recco.

My pleasure!

A week later, I got another DM from him.

What would it take for you to
go on a date with me?

What do you mean?

Come meet me in Tokyo. I'm going there
next week. I'll take you for dinner.

Are you kidding? I'm not the kind of
girl to get swept away to Tokyo.

Fair enough.

How about the next time you come
to LA, we go on a date?

Deal.

He messaged me an hour later with a screenshot of his ticket.
See you in three weeks! he said.

Now, following the post of me in my new Lululemon joggers, he DM'd me: Fuck. You're so hot.

We began messaging throughout the day, every day. I learned Evert was thirty-eight—eleven years older than me. He lived in Sweden but came to the US on business often. I avoided asking the big question for as long as I could, not wanting to put an end to this flirtation. But finally, I had to know.

Are you married? I wrote.

Yeah, he wrote. She just died.

Oh my god!

I'm just kidding. If I was married do you really think I would have asked u out?

Okay, good point

We are divorced. 2 daughters. 7+9.
My wife and I used to read all your recipes.

Really?

Yeah. I've been following U a long time

Since Evert was nine hours ahead, I'd wake up with a flurry of messages every morning. He'd send me suggestive selfies of him on the way to jiujitsu or in the steamy sauna mirror.

The morning he was to arrive in LA, I tried on a few different outfits. I wanted to look classy but sexy. I opted for a gifted white-and-blue crop top from Madewell, vintage leather sandals, and a jean skirt from Topshop. I kept my face bare and swiped the tiniest bit of gifted clean mascara on my eyelashes.

On the drive to meet him for lunch on Abbot Kinney in my Honda Fit, I played my favorite section of Bonobo's essential mix, which brought me back to my rave girl days. I felt a similar feeling of anticipation, except this time I wasn't looking to take molly in the predawn hours at Verboten. This time, I was on my way to fall in love.

I shouldn't have been surprised that the photos on his profile didn't reflect reality, but my infatuation was punctured when I saw him standing in front of our meeting spot. He was over six feet tall, but the way he hunched over his phone made him seem much smaller. He had horrible posture. He wore flip-flops, cargo shorts that were a little too big, and a ratty T-shirt. His dirty-blonde hair was swooshed back, and he had a little stubble. Then he looked up and I saw his eyes, which were even more piercing than in the photos.

"I'm all sweaty," he said as we hugged. "I've been so nervous to meet you. I can't believe that I'm here. And that you're here. My friends swore you'd ghost me or cancel on me last minute or something. They were taking bets. They all follow you too."

It was weird that Evert and his friends thought I was a celebrity. It made me feel both uncomfortable and proud. I took a whiff of him. He smelled like wood, soap, and tobacco. Upon closer look, I realized his T-shirt was actually James Perse—a $160 shirt.

We went to Gjelina Take Away for sandwiches, then drove to the beach in Malibu. We took Evert's rental car—a convertible BMW. Between the spontaneous plane ticket, the designer shirt, and the sports car, it was clear Evert had money. I later learned that he worked in property development. I wasn't impressed. In fact, it all felt a little midlife crisis to me. But I decided to have fun and enjoy it.

By the time we got to the beach, it was late afternoon and the sun had fully disappeared behind the June gloom fog. That didn't stop Evert from wanting to lay on the beach. We were the only people in the area. He picked a spot and put a blanket down. Then he wrapped a towel around himself and changed into his swimsuit. I was reminded how European Evert was in that moment, so unashamed of changing in front of a girl on a first date.

I excused myself to the public toilet to change into a reversible bikini I'd been gifted from a brand. Self-conscious about my stomach and deep belly button, I wondered if I should wear a cover-up or just walk over to Evert in my bikini. I decided to go without the cover-up. *That's the kind of brazen thing Lee From America would do,* I told myself.

We both barely touched our food, we were so nervous. We talked about our work and our families. He showed me pictures of his girls. What would it be like to date someone with kids? They were so far away. How would this fit into my life plan? Evert could somehow tell where my mind had gone.

"Do you want kids?" he asked me.

"I haven't really thought much about it," I said. "I do, I think. Yeah. Do you want any more?"

"I didn't," he said, "since I have two already."

"I see."

"Until now."

I was a little creeped out by how I'd only met this man a couple hours ago, and now he was insinuating he wanted to have children with me. But I pushed the uneasy feeling away and instead let myself feel moved and adored. I felt so comfortable around Evert. It felt like we had been together for years.

We drove back to his Airbnb. Across the dining room table were unfurled blueprints for an apartment complex he was working on in Sweden. He showed me the plans for the building and I pretended like I was interested, but all I could think about was when he was going to kiss me. I kept waiting for him to make his move, but instead we went out onto the deck and chatted some more.

Evert was telling me a story of a huge moose he saw in his backyard in Sweden. He kept talking and talking. Finally, he asked if he could kiss me. He barely got the question out before I leaned in and our lips met. After making out for a bit, we moved inside.

"Spend the night?" he asked.

I nodded.

While he was in the bathroom getting ready for bed, I again thought of how Lee From America would handle this situation. She would be bold and uninhibited. So I stripped off all my clothes and got under the covers. When Evert pulled them back and saw my naked body, he yelled out with delight, "What!!"

"Come here," I said, pulling him in with my legs.

We were inseparable for the next two weeks. He came over to my place and hung out on my bed while I worked. We went to Bar Stella in Silver Lake and Michelin-rated restaurants like Asanebo in the Valley. We went dirt biking through Topanga Canyon. I posted the experience on my stories, wondering if my followers knew that I was with a man, as this was not a usual Lee From America activity. After we finished biking, sweat pouring off us, I asked Evert if he would take a selfie with me. I wasn't ready to post it and launch our relationship. I just wanted to document our time together for myself.

The day Evert had to go back to Sweden, we slept in late at my apartment, curled up together as the light poured through the windows. I'd missed my morning post. I'd missed a few posts since his arrival. I didn't care.

"What now?" I asked, looking up at him, centimeters from his chin.

"Now," Evert said, "it's in God's hands." He smiled. "I've never felt this way about anyone, anytime in my life. Not my ex, not the girls before you. Nobody. You are the most amazing woman I have ever met."

Evert left the apartment to catch his flight. As soon as the front door shut, I burst into tears. I changed into workout clothes to go for a hike at Griffith Park. I wanted to see his plane take off from the top of the hills. When I got home, I found a hair of his on my pillow and taped it into my journal.

Twenty-One

During Evert's visit, I had neglected my following and the constant stream of content creation. My follower count had stopped growing at lightning speed. I felt anxious and guilty. I planned to take and post my first selfie in weeks, but as I stood in front of the full-length mirror, I wasn't happy with what I saw. I had put on weight from all our wining and dining. Not long before Evert's arrival, I posted about how I'd thrown out my scale. It was a very popular post. Without anything to weigh myself, I went to the closet and pulled out a pair of vintage Levi's I hadn't worn in a while. If they fit lower rise, I'd be in the clear, but if they were tight around my hips, that meant I'd put weight on. They hugged my belly and hips much tighter than I'd anticipated.

Fuck.

I still had to post something. I stood in the mirror and took thirty selfies from all different angles until I found one that was passable. As soon as I posted, I emailed the Clean Program for them to send a cleanse to arrive the next day. I needed to put myself and my body first and not let myself get fat from new love.

With the cleanse, my body soon became more defined, and I was feeling less bloated. But I was growing more obsessed about everything that crossed my lips. A follower DM'd me about how fluoride causes brain damage and how the government used it to sedate us and make us all think the same. I should have known to be skeptical about the validity of a random DM from a username like "earthy mamabear," but I was now in the habit of questioning the medical industry after getting my period back naturally through diet and stress management. I stopped using fluoride toothpaste, and on my next trip to the dentist, I asked them not to use it.

The dentist gave me an exasperated look. I got the feeling he was getting this request more and more from young people like myself, whose primary source for news and information was social media.

"Okay," he said. "If you say so."

This conscientiousness about what I put in my body made the reaction to one of my posts even more upsetting. After the dip of follower growth while Evert was in town, I soon got back to growing at a rate of one thousand per day. I booked my most mainstream client yet: Starbucks. They didn't pay much, but I figured adding such a big-name brand to my portfolio would only benefit my brand and take me to the next level. The post was for their Teavana® iced tea infusion.

I usually got close to ten thousand likes of a photo of me. This one only got six thousand. The comments were brutal.

> Ugh! Almost all their teas and coffee are not organic though ☹ which means their tea is covered in pesticides too. Do they have an option for organic??

> I researched Teavana and, apparently, they add artificial flavoring to some of their teas and their teas were tested and found to contain many pesticides, one of which is known as endosulfan, which has been linked to fertility issues and birth defects. ☹

Again, I should have known better than to assume what these people were claiming was accurate. But even being associated with something that was potentially unhealthy was upsetting—especially because I knew it undermined the all-natural personal brand I'd worked so hard to cultivate.

I texted Evert.

Don't listen to them, he responded. Starbucks is great. I can go into any Starbucks in Korea, Japan, Paris, or Dallas and get the same tasting product. They are a community hub, a wonderful business.

From then on, trying to regain the trust of my followers, I doubled down on alternative health practices like tongue scraping, dry brushing, dream journaling, the benefits of chaga mushrooms and double-filtered charcoal water, and body oiling for different doshas. I put extra effort into the PCOS content because I was extremely passionate about sharing any of my findings and tips for managing its mysterious symptoms—and it resonated deeply, performing exceptionally well. PCOS affects one in ten women and was only then getting the airtime it deserved. With periods as part of my brand, I closely monitored and shared my cycle with my followers: Hey guys, my period is late. I was stressed this month, so that's why! I knew that a thin woman posing in a bathing suit talking about how she'd conquered PCOS would draw a lot of attention, as PCOS often had the consequence of weight gain around the midsection, also known as "PCOS belly." My followers wanted to know how I'd done it—and how they could too.

I also posted about all the many supplement pills and powders I was using, with names like Dream Blend, Moon Mend, and Focus Root. I got really into adaptogens. These were blends of various medicinal plants, herbs, and roots with hard-to-pronounce names that promised healing and clarity. I was taking around fourteen servings of various blends a day. I couldn't tell which one did what, except for rhodiola—which made me feel like I'd just taken an Adderall—and triphala, a bitter-tasting blend of powders that advertised a "gentle internal cleanse." Each night around 8:30, I'd heat up a half cup of water in the kettle, place twice the recommended amount of triphala in a hand-blown glass mug—I was now wholly opposed to using plastic dishware—and stir the powder into a dark, murky concoction. I'd plug my nose and down it. I had no idea what I was drinking, but I knew it helped me produce a bowel movement every morning, and that was vital to my mood. If I couldn't poop, I'd feel bloated and get anxious about taking a selfie for Instagram. I'd also seen an Instagram post that stated "if you don't poop every day, you are constipated" and made a mental note.

PCOS-related or not, photos with me in them always performed the best. One of my most popular posts was a photo[13] of me showing off my abs on a hilltop overlooking LA. The caption was all about the importance of loving yourself. I'd had my assistant take close to two hundred different photos for the perfect one.

Around this time, I wrote in my nightly journal: *I want my followers to continue to love me and obsess over me. Keep feeding the cult.*

I confided this to Brooke. I was still doing regular breathwork sessions with her. She saw my heart chakras opening and closing and suspected that I had transferred the approval I'd always sought from my mother and father onto my followers.

"Well, don't all influencers seek approval?" I said. "That's literally the nature of our job."

"You need to think about who you're living your life for," Brooke said. "You're a bright light, Lee. People are attracted to that. You need to protect your energy."

After the session, I posted a story in which I shared these revelations with my followers.

Twenty-Two

A few weeks later, Evert returned to LA. In anticipation, I got electrolysis done on my chest and face to remove some hairs, and my entire chest broke out in whiteheads. I went to a facialist to try to pop the whiteheads, but all they could do was steam it to try to bring down the inflammation. I was so embarrassed, but I also wanted to look good, so I wore a Christy Dawn dress exposing my chest.

"Min alskling," Evert said when he arrived at my apartment. "You look beautiful."

"Don't you see my chest?" I said. I wanted to acknowledge it immediately.

"Yeah, so what?" he said and threw me onto the bed. I was always telling my followers the importance of loving yourself as you are, but I couldn't abide by the advice. I wished I could love myself in the same unconditional way Evert seemed to love me.

That night, as we cooked dinner at my apartment, Evert referred to me as his girlfriend.

"Girlfriend?" I said. "We never talked about that."

Evert laughed. "Well, what do you think we're doing?"

"Well, in America, you'd ask me. And we'd talk about it."

"Well, in Sweden, what we are doing is considered boyfriend-girlfriend. You Americans are too uptight."

He kissed me and I looked up at him. His teal eyes took me in.

"I'm a thirty-eight-year-old man. You are my girlfriend."

That dinner was a big, elaborate meal. Almost all our meals were. Evert's relationship with food was just as complicated as mine. As a child, he had been chubby with a strict, often-absent father who sent him to diet camp. As an adult, he tried to practice good habits, but the unhappiness of his marriage left him depressed and turning to food for comfort. The weight gain that followed only made him feel worse. Since his divorce, he had gotten really into fitness, especially jiujitsu. He was burning so many daily calories through the sport that he didn't have to be so mindful of his diet. It was all fuel. And for him, being in LA was a kind of vacation. He wanted to go out and have a good time and celebrate our new love and show it off in front of other people.

One night, Evert wanted to go to Bestia, one of LA's best Italian restaurants.

"Babe, we can't just walk into Bestia on a Saturday night," I said. "We'll never get a table."

"Oh, we'll *get in*," Evert said. "Just gotta give the host a little present."

"What do you mean?"

"I'll give her some money," Evert said, looking at me with a sly smile.

"That doesn't happen in real life," I said.

After valeting the car, we walked into the restaurant. As I expected, it was totally mobbed.

"We'd like a table for two," Evert said in his European accent.

The hostess gave him a condescending smile.

"I'm sorry," she said. "We don't have anything available for two tonight."

Evert looked at me and said, "Sweetheart, go to the bar and order a drink. Here is some cash. I'll be right over."

As I stood in a crowd three people deep, I watched Evert pull out a small wad of cash and lean into the hostess's ear. Now smiling genuinely and even a little flirtatiously, she nodded, took the cash, grabbed two menus, and motioned for him to follow her. Evert waved me over, and we were led to one of the most prime tables in the restaurant, heads turning as people wondered who we were to deserve such special treatment.

Holy shit. Did he really just do that?

I was so enthralled that I didn't have any qualms about Evert ordering half the menu. We were so full and tired when we got home that we both fell asleep on my bed fully clothed with just our pants unbuckled.

Because of all our dining out, I insisted we try to take a long hike every day. One day on the trail, Evert took a picture of me. I got so many comments asking who took the pic. I smiled at the secret.

On another hike, I posted a story in which Evert's shadow was visible. I got dozens of replies, all some version of: WHO IS THAT?????

The same thing happened when I uploaded a photo of two smoothie bowls: WHO IS THAT FOR????

I was excited to launch our relationship to my followers, but Evert wasn't there yet.

"I never want to be on your page, Lee," he said. "I just want to support you from behind the scenes."

I was disappointed. I didn't want to hide our love. Also, I knew it'd be good for my brand. Who would Lee From America date? Of course she'd date an attractive older man from Europe with money. But I understood the situation was complicated for Evert. Given that so many of his friends still followed me, launching our relationship would mean he'd have to have that conversation with his ex and their kids. I resolved to be patient, hoping he'd eventually come around to the idea.

My followers were not as willing to wait. I only followed a couple hundred people. One of them was Evert. My followers did some sleuthing and guessed he was my mystery man. He started receiving hundreds of follower requests each day.

They're onto us, he texted me from back in Sweden.

Just stay private, I texted back. It'll be okay.

I considered unfollowing him, but it would be more than a month before Evert's next visit to LA, and I didn't want to miss his posts, sporadic as they were. Sure, we texted directly and sent photos back and forth each day. But at this point Instagram felt to me more real than reality—more representative of one's true self. Evert seemed to share this view. Anytime I'd post a photo of myself, he'd send me a DM on the app with what he wished he could comment. Like: Beautiful, ♥♥♥. Can't believe youre mine. He could have texted this to me. His choice to instead use the app, I realize now, reflected his wanting to uphold the fantasy of me—and probably a little bit to get off on the reminder that he was a random guy who slid into an influencer's DMs and was now fucking her. Not to say his love for me wasn't genuine. I never doubted that. But the target of that love was not genuine. For him, just like for me, just like for everyone on the app, genuineness was not only undesirable, it was impossible. The app was nothing more than one of those body-distorting mirrors you'd find in a carnival fun house. It was a place for everyone to show their best selves and, when the likes rolled in, feel like the fairest of them all. But I kept logging on.

After a sold-out workshop in LA, I held a Q&A.

"I'm curious, Lee," one of the attendees said, "how did you meet your man?"

Everyone in the room laughed and then quickly fell silent, eager for my response. I knew it was pointless to deny it. I refrained from going into details, but I did answer the question.

"We met on Instagram," I said with a big smile. "How else?"

Twenty-Three

My engagement was the highest it had been yet. Each photo was garnering at least ten thousand likes per post—and frequently fifteen thousand. My stories were getting one hundred thousand views per day and my DMs were constantly flooded.

As a result, I was getting sent so much free stuff. Boxes of natural nut butters, paleo granolas, collagen, protein powders, matcha, adaptogens, teas, herbs, almond flour tortilla chips and tortillas, organic coconut butter, live-culture coconut yogurt. I didn't have room in my apartment to store it all. Not to worry: a professional closet organizer gifted me a brand-new customized shelving system, turning one of my closets into an extended pantry. When I posted[14] about the closet, Urban Outfitters Home reached out. They let me go through their catalog and pick out anything I wanted. From them and other companies, I got a new couch, new rug, new bedside table, new bedframe, new desk, new bath mat, new shower curtain. I did a home tour in the style of *MTV Cribs* and revealed my newly redecorated apartment to my audience. The more I posted these objects, the more brands reached out and the more objects I was sent. I partnered with Etsy, and then Parachute Home. Before long, every single item in my home—down to my bath drops—was gifted to me by brands.

I was also sent totally random things, like a red-light therapy device, which I posted about because I liked it. A lot of the time I had no idea how much these products actually cost. Once, I posted a story about an eight-step skin-care routine featuring various oils and serums that had been gifted to me from a natural beauty store.

"I LOVE this serum!" I said into the camera.

A few moments later, a comment popped up:

Hey Lee! Just looked it up-that oil is $155. Is it really worth it??

I didn't know because I got it for free. But I posted:

Just reading a comment here about the price of this product. They're asking if it's worth it. YEAH! It's definitely an investment, but it's so worth it.

I didn't bother telling anyone I probably would have never bought a $155 face oil. I was only using it because it was gifted.

I got a new outfit from Outdoor Voices two or three times a month. It was always exciting to see their brown earth-friendly package arrive at my doorstep. But the excitement would wear off after a few hours. Then I'd want more. I could have just asked them to send more. They never said no, especially since I was good about always posting what they sent me. But I hated to ask. I was always worried that I was being greedy and asking for too much. So I started stealing from them.

As an "affiliate ambassador," they didn't pay me but instead gave me site credit toward their clothing. For every person that used my special code, I'd get a $20 gift card automatically sent to my email address. When I shared the code, I'd often have one hundred people use it, resulting in $2,000 worth of gift cards. Looking at the card numbers, I realized that they were all different by just one number. Once I used all of them, I tried the next number up, and it worked.

I did this a few times, justifying it to myself that I deserved it, having made Outdoor Voices hundreds of thousands of dollars through affiliate sales. Then one day I received an email from someone at the company:

> Hey Lee! I hope you're having a wonderful week. Question: it looks like you've used a number of gift card codes that were intended for other ambassadors. Can you help us understand if you're having issues with your own codes or if we can help with anything on our end?

Oh shit. I'd been caught.
I responded:

> Hiiiii! Ahh, what? I am having issues with my codes, some of mine weren't working either. I'm sorry I used some of the other ambassadors' codes. I feel so bad! LMK what I can do to help the situation at all.

They responded that there would be no more auto-code sending. Instead, they'd consolidate all the credit I earned from my promotion onto one gift card and would email that single code to use. I never found out if they suspected I was stealing.

Twenty-Four

Evert finally let me launch our relationship on Instagram. He was in town for another visit, and we drove out to Joshua Tree for a weekend of hiking. He had rented another convertible—this time a Porsche. On top of a rock, we took a bunch of selfies as he held me and kissed the back of my neck, the golden-hour light hitting us just perfectly. I picked the best one and added a light filter to make the purples and oranges really pop. The caption read: Happiest with you 🌵.

Within twenty seconds of posting, the photo had four hundred likes.

WE'VE BEEN WAITING FOR THIS.

LEE, I WAS ALREADY IN LOVE WITH YOU, BUT NOW I'M IN LOVE WITH HIM TOO.

YOU HAD TO KNOW THAT THIS WOULD WIN THE ALGORITHM.

WITH ALL DUE RESPECT, THAT IS ONE FINE MAN.

Brooke DM'd me: Lookin' good from all that lovin!

In a further sign that he was looking to get more serious, he paid for us to take a two-week vacation through Europe, starting in Stockholm, where he wanted to introduce me to his two daughters. I was terrified they would dislike me. The youngest was a little shy, but the oldest immediately grabbed my hand and led us all down to a neighborhood playground. On the walk back, I watched Evert from behind as he held both of his daughters' hands. There was no hand left for me. At first I felt jealous, then ashamed for making it about me. He was such an amazing father. How did I fit in?

My insecurity was slightly allayed in Milan, when, after visiting the Duomo, we walked past Tiffany & Co.

"Do you want to go in there?" Evert asked.

I laughed nervously. "For what?"

"I don't know," he said, smiling. "A ring."

"What kind of ring?"

"What kind of ring do you think?"

In the store, Evert confidently asked for the engagement ring section. We were handed champagne flutes, and I tried on an assortment of different rings. I couldn't believe it. Was this really happening? The third ring I tried on had a large square diamond surrounded by mini diamonds. Evert found a wedding band and then slid that on top of the engagement ring. "They look good together, don't they?"

We didn't buy the rings that day, but not long after I got back to LA, Evert lavished me with yet another trip—this time to Hawaii. He didn't ask. He just texted me a photo of two round-trip tickets and said, I have never been. Always wanted to go.

So off we went to Hawaii. We ate fish tacos, walked naked on a private nude beach, and made love in our Airbnb. But I was increasingly unhappy. I was a routine junkie, and Evert's visits to LA and vacations like these threw off my routine. He didn't want me to work in Hawaii, and I didn't either, but it was my job. I felt guilty for working and guilty for not working.

My time with Evert also threw off my eating habits. My clothes fit tighter, and my breasts had grown and were sore. I was angry at Evert. His gluttonous lifestyle had made me gain weight. Every day, he wanted to go to the ice cream shop down the street. It rained much of the trip, so we ordered a lot of takeout and weren't getting outside for many hikes. On one hike we did take, I posted a photo[15] of myself on the trail but was disgusted by how big my tits looked. I didn't want to draw attention to myself in this way.

One afternoon as the rain came down outside, I lay on top of Evert and cried. I wanted to say how terrible I felt emotionally and how disgusting I thought I looked, but I was worried he would start to see me how I saw myself. He got up and started making dinner. I looked at my Apple Watch. It was only four o'clock. I was still full from the afternoon's ice cream.

Back in LA, I immersed myself in self-care: yoga, meal prep, massage, hiking, meditation. But I still felt like crap, so fatigued by late afternoon that I could no longer concentrate on work.

At my biannual ob-gyn visit, the nurse had me step on the scale and informed me I had put on six pounds in the past six months. When the doctor examined me, she noted the weight gain and, as her long, cold tool scratched at my cervix, asked me if I knew about a "balanced diet." I was offended and let her know I made healthy recipes for a living. When I told her I hadn't changed much, she said we should monitor it.

One morning, I reached for my matcha powder, the ritual that normally set my day in motion. But the vibrant green powder looked almost repulsive. I boiled some double-charcoal-filtered water and let it settle before pouring it over the matcha in my Vitamix. I added the other mix-ins that usually made my mouth water: collagen, cinnamon, and coconut butter. But as I blended and the earthy sweet scent filled the air, my stomach twisted in response. Reluctantly, I brought the gloopy, muddy mixture to my lips and took a cautious sip. The rich bitterness hit my tongue, and almost immediately a wave of nausea surged through me. I gagged, barely managing to swallow the liquid.

My hand trembled as I set the cup down. The nausea was relentless, an insistent churn. The comfort of my morning matcha was now a torment. I sat there, staring at the half-full cup, confused and frustrated, wondering what was happening to me.

That same afternoon, I reached for a fat ball from the freezer, anticipating the usual delight. As I bit into it, the texture and taste were suddenly alien. My throat tightened, and I gagged, the rich flavor turning my stomach. I spat it out into the trash. Then I rummaged through the renovated closet pantry, my mind fixated on one thing: carbs. I needed pasta, pizza, just one slice of bread, anything to quell this sudden hunger. But of course, the only thing that resembled a carb in my closet was lentil pea pasta. I'd been mostly off carbs to curb PCOS symptoms and never kept them in the house.

I sank to the floor, overwhelmed by the intensity of my cravings and the betrayal of my usual disciplined self. Tears welled up. What was my body trying to tell me?

Something inside of me told me to take a pregnancy test. It came back negative. The next morning, I took another one.

Positive.

How had my ob-gyn missed this? How had I? It wasn't a total shock. I wasn't on birth control and Evert didn't use condoms. He usually pulled out, but once or twice, he hadn't. I felt relieved that I finally had an answer for all my weird body symptoms over the last few weeks.

I sat on my yellow Aztec-inspired gifted Urban Outfitters rug and FaceTimed Evert furiously. He didn't answer. It was midnight in Sweden. I texted: WAKE UP BABE. I NEED 2 TALK.

I knew I wouldn't keep it. Evert and I had only been together for five months. We didn't live in the same country. I wasn't ready to have a kid. We couldn't agree on what our future would look like—there was still so much uncertainty.

A couple hours later, Evert woke up and checked his phone and FaceTimed me back. I told him the news.

"What? Are you kidding?"

He wasn't angry. He was smiling.

I showed him the test. Then showed him my boobs. "I told you they were bigger."

"Wow, I can't believe it. I'll do whatever you want to do."

"Well, I'm definitely getting an abortion."

"Really?" He sounded disappointed. "Well, okay, if that's what you want."

My mom happened to have a business trip in LA scheduled for that following week. We'd planned to spend as much time together as we could. I called her and told her I was still planning to pick her up from the airport. Then I told her I was pregnant. It was the second time in my life I told her that, the first being in college. It was also the second time I told her I would be getting an abortion. Just like back then, she said, "I'm so glad you told me. I'll support anything you want to do."

Just before taking the mifepristone, I started having second thoughts. What if this was my only chance at a baby? Evert and I loved each other, I had no doubt about that. I was twenty-eight. But I couldn't imagine a baby in my life. I didn't know anyone my age with kids yet. Didn't I want marriage first? Could I move to Stockholm? Could Evert and I make this work?

I called him, panicking, angry at him for not being here with me while I went through this. He didn't pick up.

I took the pill and a day later took the other pill—the misoprostol.

The bleeding began and continued for a few hours. I stayed home with a heating pad on my belly while my mom went to pick up pizza and buttery garlic knots—the only food I wanted. After I ate, I rotated from the bed to the couch, back to the bed, tensely waiting until the time the fetus would pass.

During my first abortion, I'd passed out momentarily on the toilet at the sight of the bloody mass in the bowl, briefly losing consciousness. My roommates had heard me collapse and found me on the floor, then spent the rest of the day administering me wine and Xanax. My mom wasn't so generous, offering me over-the-counter pain relievers with water.

I went to the bathroom to pee and felt something exit. I briefly moved my thigh to look into the toilet. There was a black mass, dark and solid.

"Mom!" I screamed. I didn't want to see it. I screamed for her again. "Come here! I think the fetus is in there!"

I ran out of the bathroom, back into bed. I didn't want to traumatize myself any further.

My mom went into the bathroom. When she came out, her face was white.

"I think that's it," she said.

"Are you sure? It's not the lining and the placenta?"

"I'll check."

She went back into the bathroom. Then she came back out and lay down on the bed next to me.

"That was definitely it."

"How do you know?" I said. I was now crying.

"I pushed it around with the plastic end of your toilet brush. Come here, sweetie."

My mom pulled me in, and I continued to cry. I imagined my baby, my future, dead, white, faint, angelic, in the toilet, flushed down into the LA waterways.

"I wish I was at the beach," my mom said.

The next few nights, I awoke at three in the morning, sobbing in my sleep. I had nightmares of my baby dying. I felt confused, alone, and terrified. Evert arrived a few days later. He was sweet, caring, and lovely. But he seemed to move on much faster than me. He confided in me about a fight he'd just had with his ex-wife. I envied that he still was in touch with his ex because they'd had kids. I envied that I would not be bound to him in that way. And I felt shame for my envy.

I didn't tell my followers what happened. I just kept posting sunsets and matcha.

Twenty-Five

Evert wanted me to spend more time in Sweden, so I agreed to spend New Year's Eve and the entire month of January with him. I was curious to see how living abroad might affect my business and ability to attract sponsors. Plus, I had always been fascinated by the Scandinavian way of life—their short summer nights in which the daylight seemed to stretch endlessly and the cozy, hygge-filled winter days spent indoors. I had imagined the sun in those winter months would make a grand, rapid arc across the sky, rising and setting in a swift, dramatic fashion. But as the plane touched down on the tarmac, I realized this was not the case. It was eleven a.m., yet it looked like dusk, the sky a brownish tint.

This was a problem. All my photos relied on natural light. I only took pictures in daylight and never used overhead lighting. Another issue was that my luggage got lost, and most of the Swedes were still on holiday, including the people who track down bags. My bag not only contained all the outfits I had meticulously packed for making content, but it also contained a month's worth of my adaptogens, herbs, matcha, and activated nuts.

Evert's girls were off from school and would be staying with us for my first two weeks.

"What do you want my role to be with the kids?" I asked him. "Stepmother? Girlfriend? Friend? Babysitter?"

"I don't know," he said. "Just be yourself!"

"But do I help with bedtime? Do I help discipline them, or do I spoil them?"

I was looking to him for direction. I felt helpless.

"Don't worry about it so much, min älskling," he said.

On our first full morning, we had a hike planned. I also planned to take some photos to post. Without my clothes, I borrowed Evert's black down jacket and hat. It didn't fit my body or aesthetic, but it would have to do.

The trail was beautiful: a crystalline-blue lake and long-haired moss growing up through the crevices between ancient gray stones. It was romantic and mystical, and it caused that anxious, pulling feeling in my chest that I always got when faced with something I knew would pull big numbers on Instagram. Right away I began recording for stories, zooming my camera into a bunch of wild red berries, holding them with my hand so my followers could better appreciate the scale. I stayed behind while Evert and his girls went ahead, talking in Swedish. I knew I wouldn't understand anyway. The older one, Malin, spoke good English, but Quincy was less confident. This would not be a bonding hike; this would be content.

We approached a wooden footbridge.

"Here!" I said, handing the phone to Evert to take photos[16] of me walking. Malin and Quincy watched, playing with sticks. He showed me the pictures, and I clicked my tongue.

"They're okay," I said. "Let's keep going through. I want more."

"Sounds good," Evert said. "There's a really beautiful bend in the river about twenty minutes ahead."

"Great!" I said, hastening my pace. The sun was already going down.

As we rounded a corner, Evert's oldest strayed off the path and began playing at the edge of the lake, which had frozen patches of water.

I was up on a rock doing a 180-degree camera pan of the lake.

"Malin!" Evert called. He asked her to come back up to the trail. It was Swedish, but I knew by the tone of voice what he meant. She resisted, stomping her foot on the ice repeatedly. Suddenly her entire leg fell in. Evert ran down to scoop her up. She was not hurt, more just scared, but she was all wet, freezing and crying.

"Okay, that's it," Evert called out. "Home we go!"

I put my phone down. "Home? We're going home?" I felt panic in my chest. "But what about that pretty bend?"

"She's soaked, Lee. We gotta go home. With kids, you learn that your needs come second."

My newest brand partnership was with a big meditation app I already used. The goal was to get sign-ups. Like with Outdoor Voices, I offered a discount code to my followers. The code also let the company track how many downloads I had prompted. I would do thirty consecutive days of meditating and report my experience in four videos and three posts throughout the month.

On New Year's Day, I posted a time-lapse video of me meditating in Evert's light-soaked Scandinavian living room and a six-part story introducing the app and telling my followers about my new challenge. The camera was set up perfectly, and I closed my eyes, pretending to meditate.

The next day, I received an email from the app. They wanted me to send over screenshots of my metrics. Usually, brands waited until the partnership was over to ask for screenshots. I gathered the data and sent it.

The following day, I was sitting in the kitchen, watching Evert make coffee. I refreshed my email, and saw a message from the app. They were terminating the agreement, stating that I hadn't hit their metrics.

I sat there, stunned—and slightly amused by the irony that my numbers weren't good enough for an app that promoted values like detaching from our overly materialistic society. I emailed a quick response asking them to reconsider. They emailed right back: You have not performed like others have; we can send screenshots of the other influencers' numbers for your comparison if you'd like.

Evert knew I was stressed about not having my adaptogens with me, so he took me to a health food store. The whole store was only an eighth of what Whole Foods was; they were years behind the US's domination of the healthy food space. My disappointment was obvious to Evert.

"This is why we need people like you to move to Sweden to bring healthy food here," he said.

I couldn't read any of the labels. I walked around the aisles, trying to collect things to at least make fat balls so I wouldn't have to keep eating the gluten-heavy rolls and sweets he and his kids kept around. They had no adaptogens. Most distressingly, I couldn't find any magnesium. My body had become dependent on it, relying on the mineral to coax it into regularity. Each night, I would dutifully swallow a handful of hospital-grade magnesium pills, hoping they would work their magic and help me shit. But the combination of travel-induced stress and the disruption to my routine had thrown my system into disarray, leaving me uncomfortably constipated.

As the days stretched on, my discomfort only intensified, weighing heavily on my mind and body alike. Simple tasks became arduous as I battled the relentless discomfort, my thoughts consumed by the gnawing sensation of constipation.

I did manage to find a yoga class, which I couldn't wait for. Evert and the girls dropped me off one morning. I was happy to get some space from them, desperate to feel like my old LA self—in control of my body and routine—instead of feeling locked in the house.

"I don't speak much Swedish," I told the instructor when I'd walked in.

She smiled. "No worries at all! It'll be nice and easy."

I took a spot in the back and unrolled my mat, figuring I'd just follow everyone in front of me. The entire time, the instructor spoke in Swedish, and halfway through class she switched where we faced, so that I was in the front row. She was cracking jokes in Swedish, and everyone was laughing. Were the jokes about me? I felt so alone. I was the only brunette. Everyone else was blonde—not just in the class but everywhere I went. I realized I'd always be a foreigner if I lived here. When Evert picked me up from the yoga studio, he asked how it went and I burst into tears, crying the whole way home.

He recommended I cook dinner for the two of us and the girls one night. He knew I was struggling and thought it might help to give me a purpose. I began prepping dinner at four, as there was no more daylight and cooking was the only thing left to do. The girls and Evert would have regular pasta and sauce, and I'd have bean pasta, which was gluten-free and grain-free, free of carbs and heavy on protein.

Evert was troubled by this.

"I don't like it that we don't eat the same way," he said. "I just want you to eat the same things as us."

Evert didn't like a lot of things I was doing. It seemed like the very attributes that initially drew him to me—like creating healthy recipes and staying active—were the ones he was starting to resent.

Whenever Evert came to visit me in LA, he'd be okay with my salads, matcha, and smoothies, as long as we "splurged" for dinner. Now he seemed to want to go back to his Scandi diet of coffee and pastries. Swedes spent a lot of time enjoying fika, or coffee and a little treat—usually kanelbullar, a kind of cinnamon roll. We'd typically have both three times a day, in addition to meals. I wasn't used to this much gluten. It made me feel sick. I thought running might help, but every time I'd wake up early with the intention of doing it, Evert would pull me back into bed and hold me close, telling me I should rest and not run so much.

Though I felt like he was being overly controlling, I also wondered if it was me who was having the issue with control. Maybe it was good for me to loosen up and relax my routine. But I was depressed, constipated, and increasingly claustrophobic from being holed up in the house with so little daylight.

I felt the darkness of the Swedish winter directly conflicting with my light, bright, and happy LA brand.

The way I usually dealt with these kinds of emotions was to go on stories and talk about it with my followers, but I couldn't because the house was commandeered by Evert and the girls. My brain was fixated on content I should post, but there was nowhere quiet or private enough for me to record. I had to seize opportunities when I could. While the kids and Evert ran an errand or headed to the playground, I'd opt out and hop on stories to check in with my audience or film myself dancing.

A couple weeks into my time there, I posted a sunset from Evert's backyard. Instead of talking to Evert about my emotions, I put it into a caption, sharing the challenges and rewards of traveling, acknowledging the privilege but also the difficulties like the lack of control, disruption of routines, and dealing with the unfamiliarity, especially around food. I also highlighted the growth and self-discovery that I hoped was coming along with this.

Later that night, Evert said, "I just read the caption you put up on social."

"Yeah?" I said.

Evert looked at me, then looked back at the TV.

"I'm going to bed," I said. Then I slept for fourteen hours. I woke up groggy at nine a.m. to more dark clouds and fog.

At one point during the month, I asked Evert, "Is this it?" I wasn't sure domesticity at this level was for me.

"Yes, Lee," he said. "This is it. What did you expect?"

More attention, I thought. More freedom. More joy. But I didn't say any of these things. Instead, as usual, I retreated to my phone and social media. Scrolling through all the other LA influencers' vibrant egg-yolk breakfasts and sunny beach days made me miss the US.

Adidas emailed with the offer of a modeling gig and a sponsored post. I would have to leave Sweden early.

"How much are you getting for it?" Evert asked.

"Fifteen thousand," I said.

"So I'm worth fifteen thousand?"

I was exasperated but also tired of compromising.

"I need to work," I said. "It doesn't mean I don't still love you."

On the plane back to LA, I felt like I could exhale for the first time in weeks. Somewhere over Greenland, I put on a face mask and uploaded it to Instagram, saying how great it felt to practice self-care thirty thousand feet up.

I then realized it was MLK Day. Though I tried to keep my posts free from politics and news, my followers expected some acknowledgment of these topics. For instance, the day after the Las Vegas music festival shooting, my feed was full of people posting statistics about gun violence and gun laws in America compared to other countries. I didn't know anything about gun laws, and there were already enough thoughts and prayers. So I posted a photo of my breakfast just as I did every day: a bowl of overnight oats with the recipe in the caption.

Angry comments flooded in.

> Ur not going to say anything about what happened in Vegas?

> Wow. 60 people dead due to gun violence and ppl really be posting oatmeal. I hate food bloggers cc @Leefromamerica

I panic-deleted the oatmeal picture and spent the rest of my morning researching gun laws and nonprofits I could link to in my post. When I did post, the tenor of the comments changed.

Thank you for your words.

Now, on the flight back to LA, I posted a mirror selfie[17] highlighting my skin-care routine on the plane, including an orange face mask.

On my stories I uploaded a photo of the plane window with the quote: If you can't fly then run. If you can't run then walk. If you can't walk then crawl. But whatever you do, you must keep moving forward. —Dr. Martin Luther King, Jr.

Twenty-Six

Back in LA, I homed in on my routine to get back to my body and myself. I went to bed before nine and started waking up naturally around 4:45. I'd read somewhere online that if you woke up after first light, you'd have a drowsy day. I'd also read somewhere online that all the most successful people woke up early: Martha Stewart, Michelle Obama, Tim Cook.

After scraping my tongue, I'd fixed myself a cup of hot double-charcoal-filled water with lemon, making sure to drink slowly as to be fully conscious of each sip as it traveled down my esophagus. Then I got dressed in my workout gear, usually an Outdoor Voices or Adidas matching set. I always wore matching workout sets. There was a reflective glass at Equinox where I would take a boomerang of me walking toward the glass to show my followers that I was working out and looking cute. On the way to Equinox, I listened to Deepak Chopra's *Soul of Healing Affirmations* on Spotify. After my workout, I came home and showered, dabbed the moisture off my skin with my gifted Parachute waffle towels, brushed my skin with my gifted dry brush, then rubbed my body in gifted sesame oil. I then lit palo santo, pulled a tarot, meditated for forty-five minutes, and journaled. Finally, around ten or so, I logged on to Instagram and started work.

I did two twenty-one-day cleanses back-to-back. I got rid of gluten, dairy, soy, peanuts, and sugar. I paid Brooke the first half of an $8,000 coaching package, which included breathwork, moon circles, and unlimited text support. I didn't even think about the money. The meditation app reneging was an anomaly. The money was flowing in. The next time Evert was in town, I took him with me to buy a new car.

I was thinking a Subaru or a Volvo. Evert was not having it.

"Audi, babe," he said.

We drove to Audi Beverly Hills. Inside the showroom, the air was filled with the scent of new leather and polished metal. The salesman was around my age and showed me a white, barely used A4.

"Would you like to take it for a test drive?" the salesman asked. His smile lingered. I saw Evert's jaw tighten visibly. I nodded.

We took the car out for a spin, and I squealed with delight at how effortlessly it glided down the LA streets. I knew it was the one for me, and I said as much to the salesman in the passenger seat. Evert, sitting in the back, gave me a dirty look in the rearview mirror.

As we walked back into the dealership, Evert said under his breath, "You shouldn't have sounded so excited about the car while driving it. Now they know you *want* it. Trust me, I know what I'm doing with cars."

Inside his office, the salesman put the paperwork together amid friendly banter. Evert stood off to the side, arms crossed, eyes narrowed, fuming silently.

I was so proud. My career was doing so well that I had more than enough cash in the bank to buy a luxury car outright. But Evert couldn't resist spoiling my happiness.

"This guy's a farce," he said when the salesman stepped out to get something signed by his manager.

Evert was acting like he was the one buying the car.

"That guy wants to fuck you," he said. Immediately I recalled Zev saying the same thing to me years before in New York. I realized I could no longer be in this relationship.

Later that night, I told him I wanted to break up.

"What?" he said.

"Things haven't been the same for me since Sweden," I said. "This is what's best for me right now."

Evert tried to talk me out of it, but I'd been talked out of breaking up with too many exes. I stayed firm in my decision.

Evert had planned to be in LA for a month. He'd made arrangements with work and childcare. Rather than cut his trip short and have to go home and explain why, he decided to remain in LA and stay in a hotel.

A couple nights later, lying in bed crying, I scrolled my phone over to the camera and snapped a few pictures, face red, tears streaking down my cheeks. I posted it to stories with the caption:

> I'm goin through it. I could be so tempted to bury myself in work, food, exercise, shopping, booze, whatever it is. I've done that all before in previous break ups. But I'm not doing that this time. Most of the time I feel confident and clear about the future. But suddenly, a weight of sadness sinks in. thoughts like, 'will I ever find love again?' even float through my mind. I understand they hold no truth, but they still wisp by. I grieve for what was lost, the way I thought my life would pan out. that may be one of the hardest parts of the end of a relationship.

I got tons of DMs, which let me know this type of content[18] was good enough for the grid. For the next couple days, I posted breakup content. Every time I cried, I ran to the spot in my apartment with the best natural light to photograph my tears.

After several of these posts, Evert texted me:

> Please don't post about our breakup. My friends follow you and I haven't told them yet.

I wanted to text back: This is my job, and I can do what I want! I hated that Evert was still watching my stuff. But I knew if I blocked him he'd just create a finsta, an Instagram account under an anonymous handle. Even so, I still had love and sympathy for him, and I promised not to post so frequently about the breakup.

A week later it was my birthday, and Evert had an intricate, expensive bouquet delivered from my favorite LA florist on Instagram. He asked if he could come over, and I agreed. We slept together, and afterward, he showed me his new watch: a shiny silver Rolex with a blue face.

"I got this after you broke up with me," he said. "A little emotional shopping. You made me do it."

I made him do it? This seemed like one more example of his immaturity, and it was enough to convince me that I'd been right about the breakup. When Evert flew back to Sweden, we were officially over and stopped communicating. But even then I couldn't escape him.

One morning I opened Instagram to find a DM:

> Hi Lee. It's your follower, Sara. I'm a huge fan. I live in Sweden. I just wanted to let you know I just saw Evert on the street with some people. I gave him a hairy eyeball on your behalf!!!

A couple months later, I got DM from another follower—a smaller wellness influencer who specialized in yoga. She lived on an island off the coast of Spain. We'd been DMing and she'd even invited me to come visit her.

Hey Lee. Is this ur ex?

She sent me a screenshot of Evert's request to follow her. Umm yes, I replied.

Kind of strange that he followed me, right?

At first I thought she had reached out in an attempt to comfort me—to show me I shouldn't be so heartbroken if Evert clearly wasn't. But the more I thought about it, the more I wondered if it was a competitive thing, and she was trying to make me jealous.

I was feeling more and more uncertain about the sincerity of the influencer friends I was making through the app. Perhaps because I was uncertain about my own sincerity toward those friends.

One of these was Ruby, an influencer from Sante Fe who was steadily growing her following. We'd hung out in person a few times. I went to visit her for her birthday, and she came over to LA to stay with me at a free Airbnb I got in the desert in exchange for posting. Our hangs almost always included mushrooms. We never revealed that to our followers, though they might've surmised from the trippy photos we posted.

I really liked Ruby, but I felt competitive with her. I had more followers and better engagement, but I knew at any time she could surpass me. Before driving out to the desert, we stopped at Erewhon to pick up groceries for the next few days. Erewhon was the luxury grocery store chain where all the influencers went to shop—and more so to be seen. I always made sure to be well dressed when I went to Erewhon in case any followers stopped me. That day I wore a taupe cowboy hat, a cropped denim white cutoff shirt, and red Jesse Kamm sailor pants. I was stopped by three followers. Ruby was only stopped by one. I had won.

I would have felt more assured in friendships from my preinfluencing days, but I'd lost nearly all of those—including a friend who cut me off after I did a sponsored post for a fertility tracker as a form of natural birth control. This friend was one of the few people I'd confided in about my abortion. After the post, she texted:

> dude I can't take it anymore, you're so full of shit. How can you preach to people this method who take your word for everything you do when you got pregnant while using it?

I wrote back that I hadn't been using the tracker when I got pregnant, but it didn't matter. She was done. The fucked-up thing is that I was less concerned about the friendship ending than I was about the possibility she might post about my abortion and perceived hypocrisy in the comments.

Twenty-Seven

It had been three months since I last spoke to Evert. We had blocked each other, but I was feeling incredibly lonely and decided to unblock him. He noticed almost instantly (I always suspected he had multiple finstas to track me) and FaceTimed me.

We talked for ten minutes. It was wonderful to hear his voice. He told me he was traveling to Croatia the next day for a business trip. He spoke about the trip the way he often did—lightly boasting to entice me—describing the private villa perched atop a hill, the kind you could only rent if you knew someone. It came with a private chef who prepared fresh local seafood each night and a stone pool that overlooked the ocean.

He was going to Croatia to look at stone—he exported a lot of it from the Balkans for his properties—and bringing along his recently divorced friend, whom he'd roped into working for him to help him out of a rut.

They'd look at stone, eat well, sleep like kings, and snorkel in the Adriatic water.

He asked me to join him. I couldn't resist and said yes. When I got off the phone, I went straight to his profile, now that he had unblocked me. Under his tagged photos, a girl with the username @laine had posted some pictures of him.

I immediately FaceTimed him back.

"You slept with someone!"

"How did you know?" Evert asked.

"Your Instagram. She took some photos of you during your 'magical Malibu stay.'"

He let out a sigh. "I met her at a coffee shop in Malibu and she got us drugs. Yes, we slept together, but that was it."

I'd not slept with a man, or even dated one, since we'd broken up. I couldn't. And I couldn't understand how Evert was taking drugs and fucking a girl—one who, according to her bio, was twenty-five. He was thirty-nine.

And yet I still went to Croatia—a nearly twenty-four-hour trip from LA. We traveled by charter boat to a small island off the coast, then headed up a hill by foot in the dark to our private stone villa, surrounded by dense trees, the island alive with the clicks of crickets. Evert told me he'd put his friend up in a different hotel so that we could be alone. That night, my longing for him was so great that I climbed on top of him, fully clothed, and came just by rubbing against him.

At dawn, I awoke to a chorus of cicadas and the scent of wild lavender and sage drifting through the open window. The morning light revealed a stunning view: rolling hills covered in wildflowers and cypress trees, the shimmering sea beyond with picturesque sailboats and villas along the coast. It was like stepping into a painting.

We sat on the terrace, sipping rich, aromatic coffee. We ate fresh fruit plucked from the trees surrounding the villa—juicy peaches, sweet figs. It was a perfect, tranquil start to the day.

Evert's phone dinged, and he looked at it. I saw his face change and knew something was up.

"Is that the girl?"

He put the phone down and looked at me.

"Yes."

"I thought you ended it."

"I didn't end it. I didn't want her to get hurt. I just stopped responding. I ghosted."

"Are you fucking kidding me?"

I felt like such an idiot. I'd just traveled an entire day to be here, and his little twenty-five-year-old fuckgirl was texting him. I stormed out.

"I'll block her!" he yelled after me. "I promise! Lee!"

I went for a run and posted it to my stories, smiling for the camera as I dashed up and down ancient staircases covered in honeysuckle bushes. I wandered around the island, which had no cars and was walkable in less than an hour. I walked back to the villa to change into my bathing suit and headed to the beach, continuing to ignore Evert. He followed me.

What was I going to do, leave the island? How? Evert had hired the boats to get us to and from the mainland. I decided to let it go and try to enjoy my time there.

I had Evert take some pictures of me on the rocks. The photo[19] racked up twenty-five thousand likes.

WOW!! She's in Croatia!

Maybe she's back with her Swede

No way!

I didn't want to tell my followers that I was back with Evert, but I wanted @laine to know. Evert mentioned he'd told her about me. If she was like most girls, she'd check my page.

One afternoon, as Evert and I walked around the island, a man about my age approached me.

"Are you Lee From America?" he asked.

Evert laughed. "You know you've made it when you get recognized on an island where only Euros come to vacation. You are the only American here."

By the end of the trip, I'd forgiven him.

"If we are going to make this work," I said, "you need to adapt to my lifestyle. Also, no talk of kids, babies, marriage, or moving in. Let's start from scratch."

He agreed. I signed him up for my cycle-syncing app so that when I was on my period, he'd get an email reminder to give me space and support. I made him promise to read books about love languages and *The Four Agreements*, to go to therapy and to work on himself. I told him I'd be on a diet whether he liked it or not.

That last item was the most difficult for him.

The next time Evert was in LA, he brought a printed packet of documents about orthorexia. I'd encountered the term once or twice but didn't think much of it. It hadn't come up during my treatment in high school or with any specialist after.

"It's an eating disorder where a person overly fixates on eating healthy food. You have all the signs. You've cut out entire food groups. You won't eat anything that comes packaged. You meal prep constantly. You're always constipated. Perfectionism."

"My business is run on eating healthy," I said. "I love to be healthy. If you can't handle that—"

"But your healthy lifestyle is affecting everyone around you. Don't you see? It's affecting our relationship. I used to be bullied for being fat. And around you, I feel the same kind of shame. I feel judged, like I'm doing something wrong if I don't do a cleanse or eat bean pasta or whatever the heck you do. Why can't we eat healthy sometimes, unhealthy others?"

I knew there was some truth to what he was saying, but I was not ready to admit it.

"Evert, if you want to stay together, you need to accept that I am healthy. I don't like to eat out four times a week. I don't like to eat too much. Stop pressuring me."

He let it go. But while I couldn't admit it to him, I did bring it up in my next session with Brooke.

"I'm skipping meals," I told her, and shared my experience of disordered eating in high school.

"It sounds like you are really stressed-out," she said. "What does your inner child need?"

"I don't know. I'm scared I'm going to relapse."

"When you go home, do some tapping for rewiring."

Twenty-Eight

My grandmother Tilly lived between Florida and Vermont. I always felt fond of Tilly. She was an elegant woman: She taught my sister and I how to curtsy and wear white gloves to the fancy parties she and my grandfather would throw. One day I called her and recorded it with my phone's camera.

"Tilly, hi!" I said, extra loud so the camera could hear me.

"Oh, Leels, hello dear," she said in her little drawl.

"I just wanted to call and say hello. I miss you. I'm thinking of you."

I was saying it to Tilly, but really I was saying it to the camera.

"Oh dear, it means so much to me."

I didn't tell Tilly I was recording our call, or that I would be posting it to Instagram. I uploaded it onto stories with the caption: Reminder to call your grandparents today!

Though I would occasionally integrate my family into my content, whether through throwback photos or on trips home for the holidays, they didn't understand my career and why it required me to share so much of my personal life and why I had adopted this all-organic new-age persona.

My work had even been featured in the *Wall Street Journal*, a newspaper Tilly and my grandfather Bunky had been subscribed to for decades, but my family only noted it with tepid pride.

This came to a head at my sister's wedding. Lexie and her fiancé, Peter, had been together for about six years. I loved Peter and was so happy for them, and couldn't wait to celebrate. However, in the weeks leading up to the wedding, Lexie asked if I was going to shave my armpits. She'd seen a selfie I'd posted online in which I was showing off my new all-natural look, and she was not okay with it. Neither were my parents.

The morning of the wedding, I was back home in Connecticut, upstairs in the bathroom getting ready. My father knocked on the door.

"Hey, Lee-Lee." He was still in his pajamas, holding a coffee mug. "Will you please shave your armpits? Please. It's Lexie's big day, and she—"

"Dad, it's my body. I don't tell you what you should do with yours. Am I telling you what to do with the hair around your penis?"

My dad stared at me in shock.

"I'm out of this," he said and walked downstairs.

My mom came in next.

"Lee, will you please, please, please shave your armpits for the wedding."

"I'm not going to do it. This is my body."

"Lee, please. I'm going to ask you one more time."

We kept arguing, and she began to wear me down. My family wouldn't see it my way. And they would never let me live it down.

I went to the bride herself.

"Lexie, Mom and Dad keep asking me to shave my armpits. It's hurting my feelings they won't accept my body the way it looks. Is it really that important to you?"

"It really is, Lee," she said. "For the pictures. Just think of the pictures."

This was an argument that I could understand.

I went into the bathroom, took my razor, and removed all my hair.

Distraught over what I saw as compromising my principles, I texted my cousin who had a bit of a party streak.

"Do you have any mushrooms?" I asked.

"Yup," she said.

I cried at the altar, watching Lexie kiss her husband, and the whole church burst into applause. It made me realize the tenuousness of my relationship with Evert. He recently bought an apartment in Stockholm. Not long after he had texted me:

> Hi Lee. I know this may be hard to swallow. But you need to move to Europe. I want you to move to Stockholm next summer. It's the only way we can be together. I want to be with you. I can't move to America until my kids are at least 18. That's ten more years. I don't want to financially commit to renting a place there. It just makes sense for you to come here. I know that's a lot to swallow. Think about it.

After the ceremony, we headed to the beach for the reception. It was a beautiful September night on the Long Island Sound, and the tent stood about a hundred feet from the water's edge. As I stood at a high-top table eating coconut rock shrimp, a family friend who followed me on Instagram came over and lifted my arm.

"Let me see the hair!" she yelped.

When she saw nothing, she was disappointed.

"But you had armpit hair in your photos last week!"

This reminded me that I had yet to get a photo of my sister and me that I could post. I went and found her and pulled her aside.

"Lexie, I know you're doing all these professional photos, but I also want one with my phone for my Instagram."

My mom overheard and barged in.

"Lee, we've got over forty family members and wedding party photos to get to," she said. "Your photo is not a priority."

"Stop getting in the way of our conversations!" I snapped. The sunset was waning, and the vision I had for our photo was singed in my mind, as was always the case. I had to get this shot. When else could I get it?

My mom and Lexie knew it was quicker to relent than to fight. Mom took the photos: ten, twenty, thirty. We kept smiling.

"Okay, Lex, you gotta go!" my mom said.

"No, a few more!" I yelled.

In the bathroom of the country club, my cousin and I reached into her crinkly sandwich bag of dried mushrooms. My maid of honor toast was scheduled for an hour from now—and the mushrooms would kick in right after. My timing was precise.

As I rose to give the speech, every color and sound and smell was heightened: the chandeliers twinkling overhead; the bouquets of roses, ranunculus, and hyacinth; the clink of champagne glasses; the faces and chatter of our family and friends. I started things light and got some laughs. But then tears streamed down my face as I shared how much joy it brought me to see Lexie find someone so devoted to her. She was crying too, and after I finished, we embraced.

I spent the rest of the night dancing and eyeing my brother-in-law's cute groomsmen, wondering why none of them would hit on me. I was partly hoping someone would present me with molly or coke like the old days.

The next morning, head cloudy from my mushroom trip, I posted the photo[20] of me and Lexie with a caption about watching your older sister do everything first.

One of the first comments was from a follower with the username "creatingnelly":

> Why did u conform to societies rules and shave ur armpits for the wedding?!

Twenty-Nine

The next time Evert came to LA, I asked him to stay at a hotel, citing the need for space. He refused, saying, "If we can't live together in your tiny apartment, how can we live together anywhere else?"

I went to see a tarot reader and asked her if I should break up with Evert. At this point, I was looking everywhere for answers on how to live my life: tarot, my moon ritual planner, astrology, my life coach. I opened my tea bags and checked the inspirational quotes on the tag. I scoured Yung Pueblo's and Rupi Kaur's Instagram feeds like they were ancient scrolls, decoding the captions for a sign. I was desperate for anything to provide the guidance I sought.

The tarot cards revealed a seven of swords. This often shows up when you are doing something you know deep down isn't that great, but you're trying to justify your actions to yourself.

Later that day, at the beach in Santa Monica, Evert said, "When we move in together, I think I should be a stay-at-home dad and take care of our kids."

"Evert," I said. "This needs to end."

He laughed. "Are you breaking up with me again?"

We had done this so many times now. And usually, we made up

with sex. Like on the flight back from Croatia. As we fixed our seat belts, I leaned over to kiss Evert on the cheek and noticed two women around my age, a blonde and a brunette. They were pretty. Evert kissed me back, then looked to where my eyes were, and saw the girls.

Evert squeezed my hand and flipped through some movies.

"What do you want to watch?" he asked.

I stayed silent. He nudged me.

"Lee?"

My brain was going haywire. Did he find them more attractive than me? Was he going to leave me for these girls? Would he fuck them on molly, then keep texting them on our next trip? Did he want them more than me? Did he want me at all?

"Do you want to fuck those girls?" I blurted out.

"What?! What are you talking about, Lee?"

"I saw you look at those girls."

"Of course I don't want to fuck them," he said.

I kissed him hard, deeply. He put a blanket over me and began fingering me until I came, quietly, somewhere over the Atlantic.

Now here on the beach in Santa Monica, though, I knew there would be no make-up sex. I looked down at the sand, feeling terrible.

"Yes," I said. "For real this time. No more getting back together. I'm tired of seesawing."

I had tickets to go to Sweden for the following week. "I'm not going to come," I said. "This is too much of a distraction to my work. I want to work on my work. I don't want to work on us."

The next morning before he left my apartment for the airport, we hugged goodbye. In my bedroom he left a note:

I understand. I'm sorry I pushed you. I'll always care about you.

I meant it when I said I wanted to work on my work. I invested more money into my business than I ever had. I hired a design agency to redo my blog and logo. In addition to my assistant, I hired a woman named Dalen as my business coordinator, with a focus on my new ambition of expanding workshops. So far, all the workshops I'd done had sold out. If I could grow this aspect of my business, I wouldn't have to be so reliant on brand partnerships for income.

Dalen quickly set up a workshop tour of the Pacific Northwest, with stops in Portland, Seattle, and San Francisco. She booked my travel and accommodations and secured brand partnerships for all the items in the goodie bags each attendee would receive. The bags typically contained items like a coupon to Outdoor Voices, a handmade ceramic bowl, collagen, matcha, a year-ahead agenda, adaptogens, protein bars, skin-care products from CAP Beauty and Moon Juice. All in all, the bag's contents were worth well over $250.

As announcement day for the tour approached, I worried about the ticket price increase.

My first workshop after moving to LA was around $85. Over the years, I'd raised ticket prices to around $150. Each one sold out immediately. This told me that the demand was there.

My following had grown significantly since my last workshop, and I wanted to focus on aspects of my business that were not beholden to corporate sponsorships. Workshops were much more fulfilling, allowing me to connect with my community IRL, but they were also a big investment. I always rented the most beautiful, light-filled spaces, covered travel for my team, event insurance, materials, and ensured everyone was paid fairly. These workshops took months to plan, and I wanted to profit off them. Most of the time I barely broke even.

We decided to raise prices this time, with general admission tickets starting at $350 and the VIP option going up to $650. The VIP ticket included not only access to the workshop, but also a seat at an intimate dinner with me and a few other VIP ticket holders, higher-value gift cards, and a limited-edition tarot deck tucked into each gift bag.

I confided my concern over the steep ticket price to Brooke. After I broke down the numbers for her, she said it was not unreasonable.

"You are doing this for so many reasons," she reminded me. "Not just for money. But so that you can connect with your followers and give them an experience in real life. You need that to keep going. Do not attach yourself to the outcome."

Compared to the thousands of dollars I was paying her as my life coach to deliver generic reassurance like this, the workshop fee seemed like a bargain.

For a couple weeks, I teased my followers about a big announcement. That morning, I woke up at five a.m. and journaled a few affirmations:

> My intuitive superpowers communicate through me with clear visions, messages, voices, and spirit guides. They let me know when something is not right. My intuition is strong and clear. It helps guide me to where I am in the present moment, which is exactly where I need to be. I trust my gut. I am a business. I am an employer. I hold all the answers inside of me. My failures do not define me. Growing and stretching is uncomfortable, but that is how you change.

Finally, it was time to post. Wanting to make sure none of my followers missed it, I did a trifecta: grid, story, and live. The grid post[21] was a photo of me in jeans, barefoot, legs crossed, sitting on my IKEA kitchen cart holding a matcha next to a Vitamix. In the live, I cheerily detailed what the three-hour workshops would entail.

"There will be cooking tutorials for pumpkin fat balls and a creamy coconut butter adaptogenic drink, seminars on mindful eating and Ayurvedic practices, tips on cultivating true self-love and self-care, and so much more that I don't cover online."

The comments started flooding in.

> This is amazing!!!

Let's go!!!

This sounds unreal.

Ticket bought!

Feeling great about the response and relieved the prices weren't deterring people, I closed the app and set my phone aside. That lasted about five minutes. I craved the validation. I wanted to bask in every ecstatic comment from my followers. In that five minutes, though, the sentiment had changed and the comments had taken a turn.

> The 'wellness' industry is a billion-dollar biz and y'all are just finding this out. Support women but the cost of these workshops is ludicrous freelancer capitalism

> Wow, I could go to Morocco for this price.

> This is why Corey is better, she isn't money hungry or fake like Lee.

Corey was another So-Cal health blogger with an equally big following. She loved palo santo, God, "thiq" smoothies, her kids, and Drake. She was just as ambitious as I was. We were friendly with each other, but I suspected she viewed me as competition. She was always gossiping about other influencers to me, which made me realize that she was probably doing the exact same thing behind my back.

It wasn't my first experience with negative comments. It was all part of being a successful influencer. And usually the comments were so ridiculous I could shake them off. For instance, once after I went to an infrared sauna in Brentwood, I took some selfies in my car, parked on the side of the street. I posed with one foot on the gas, the other leg bent on the driver's seat. I posted the photo[22] with the goofy caption: Most comfortable way to drive a car, no questions asked.

I immediately got comments like:

With no seatbelt? YEAH, so cool. Eyeroll.

This is dangerous and irresponsible to advertise when you have hundreds of thousands of followers.

You can misalign your SI joint from driving like this.

If you drive with one leg up and hit the car in front of you, your leg will compact into itself and become decapitated. It's just much safer to drive with both feet down. You have the ethical responsibility with a big platform to show safe driving.

While it was easy to dismiss this kind of reaction, the negative comments still registered. I got more than thirteen thousand likes on that car photo and more than two hundred positive comments, but the few negative ones still stung. That was a central function of the app, after all: to heighten your insecurity and make you feel less than, so that, with your self-confidence demoralized, you'd use the app even more—to aspire to all the other people who seemed better than you and hopefully prove your self-worth through more posting. I understood this implicitly, but that couldn't deter me from feeding the beast.

I tried to focus on the positive comments on my workshop post, but they were quickly outnumbered by the negative.

Uhhh . . . $350??? For 2 hrs? Who is this workshop FOR?

Michael Pollan will cook for me for $50. You are NOT spreading inclusivity.

Whooooo do you think you ARE?

I felt all my muscles clench. My breathing sped up. I felt dizzy and began to shake. I felt the blood leave my face and fingers and rush to my stomach, only to leave that too.

I was empty.

My phone continued to buzz.

It got worse. The comments were now coming from verified users: celebrities, comedians, chefs. All of them expressing disgust and disdain.

Then the comments turned to white privilege.

> A white girl doing a workshop inspired by matcha (Japanese) and ayurveda (Indian) and charging $350???? This workshop is for white people.

> Your workshops are only priced to include massively affluent people; they are not serving the community. You are perpetuating the idea that wellness is only avail to rich/white/cis women.

I began to panic.

I called Dalen. "I can't handle this," I said. "I am deleting Instagram from my phone. Can you log on and put out any fires?" This is why I'd hired help. I now had a team who could handle pushback for me.

"Do you want me to delete comments?" Dalen asked.

"Yes," I said. "It's okay to block people and delete comments if they are sassy or mean."

I gave Dalen my password, turned my phone to silent, then headed outside in a pastel two-toned Outdoor Voices set for a walk. The sun shone bright, and no clouds were in the sky, but the beauty of the day didn't register. I barely made it half a mile before checking my phone. I couldn't resist.

I had a text from my mom and dad:

Hi Lee. Just wanted you to know we're thinking about you. We saw what's going down on the page. People are so mean. We love you. Here if u want to chat.

I had a text from a high school friend:

Hey girl. U OK??? Saw ur IG.

I even had a text from some random girl from college I hadn't been in contact with for years:

Damn wtf is going on? People r crazy.

I called Dalen. "How's it going?" I asked.
"Well, all the VIP tickets sold out," she said.
"How about general admission?"
"They're selling a little slower than we hoped. But . . . uh . . ."
"What?" I asked.
I could hear Dalen take a deep breath.
"People are calling you racist," she said. "I absolutely deleted those comments."

Clearly, I wasn't going to be able to rely on Dalen to handle this. I hurried back to my apartment, reinstalled the app, and read through the hundreds of comments, most of them negative. One of the comments Dalen deleted had been made by a person of color, who then created a new account and posted that I had silenced the BIPOC community.

COMMENT DELETER!

Why are you silencing negativity?

Can you not handle it? You should. You're an influencer.

I tried to tell myself this was actually *a good thing*. The announcement was spurring a conversation around wellness, accessibility, inclusivity, and privilege. These were all things that needed to be discussed. I thought about posting a story saying as much, but Dalen urged me not to, saying that might only inflame the situation. Instead, she suggested we donate the proceeds from two tickets per city to a local charity.

Much as I wanted all this to go away, I didn't like the idea of donating my hard-earned revenue just to placate total strangers on the internet who knew nothing about me or my business. I already gave so much away for free. My followers didn't pay for my online content. Giving away my money to charity was an admission that my ticket pricing was wrong and that I was not worthy of that dollar amount. I thought about the thousands of young women who looked to me as an entrepreneur. What would it look like to them if I let the criticism cow me?

I texted Brooke and asked for reassurance.

Women who are jealous and hurt react with anger when they see other women succeeding or making money, she responded. Because they believe they cannot achieve that for themselves. Taking the woman down is easier than taking a positive action for themselves to get where you are.

It was probably true, but it was not the time for spiritual euphemisms.

This was an emergency. I felt like I was about to lose everything. And at the end of the day, of course I cared about inclusivity.

I called a friend and fellow business owner in the wellness space in LA and asked her advice. "Lee, many women have been in a situation like you," she said. "The problem is you are trying to appeal to everyone. Look at Lacy Phillips. She promotes luxurious things, and her work is expensive. But she owns it and doesn't apologize for it. Either own it and don't look at the criticism or change your whole business and make it more accessible. You can't be both. Right now, you are trying to be budget and luxurious. It won't work."

This made sense as a long-term consideration, but it didn't help me resolve the immediate issue. By that point, it was late into the evening. I decided to sleep on it. But sleep proved impossible, and in the morning I was even more anxious. I figured I'd try just going back to my normally scheduled posting. I made carrot top pesto and soft scrambled eggs on toast and posted it with a recipe. The first comment read:

> I have to agree with your critics. 650 for a workshop? I'll keep my money, thanks.

Another comment read: Yas girl go off. Keep posting about avocado toast when ur being accused of white privilege.

I was also getting bombarded with DMs. I had 250 in the last twelve hours. Half were messages of support. Don't listen to the haters, keep doing what you're doing. Anyone who owns a business understands you need to make a profit! The other half expressed the same vitriol of the comments. LOL U got to be kidding me with these prices. You are fucking ridiculous. I will be unfollowing you now. You are NOT who you say you are. The story was spilling out of the app. Someone DM'd me an article written about the workshop fallout on a private blog. I opened and read every DM. I don't know why. I don't know what I was searching for. But I kept opening them.

I received an email from Evert: Let me know that you're okay plzzzz. I wasn't sure if he meant okay from the breakup or the workshop drama. I wanted desperately to respond to him and to lean on him for support and ask his opinion. But I resisted. Things were already messy enough.

Dalen told me that Evert had also messaged her to check up on me. Then my mom started coming to my defense in the comments. That's when I realized I had to do whatever I could to shut this down. As much as I appreciated her support, I didn't want my parents defending me. I worried they'd be canceled too.

I decided to go with Dalen's donation idea. I posted to the grid: We planned on launching our donation program next week, but clearly this can't wait. In light of comments on yesterday's post, I'm excited to share we're now donating 2 tickets per city. This was a lie, of course.

For this post, I used a photo of myself in a field outside of LA that I'd taken months prior. I wore a white felt hat and a fuzzy camel-colored zip-up, and held to my chin a bouquet of three orange California poppies. I figured it would be the perfect photo[23] to show my humanity: a makeup-free, freckle-faced girl in nature.

Within seconds, comments poured in:

Hi Lee. I've alerted the local authorities of your illegal crime. They know your address and you will receive a hefty fine in the mail. I suggest you delete this to avoid further penalty as this promotes criminal behavior.

Ew gross white woman who picks sacred flowers.

Wow . . . lol u call urself a wellness influencer and then kill nature. COOL.

#LEEVEAmerica

I didn't realize picking poppies was illegal in California. Now I was getting attacked for a whole new thing.

I tried to go about my day and keep to my routine. In the early evening, I went to the gym. I normally loved Equinox's fluorescent lights for how flattering they were in photos. Now they scared me.

I felt exposed. Was a follower here? Would someone confront me in person? I turned around and left.

As I drove home, darkness settled over the city. My heart rate had now been in overdrive for over thirty-five hours. I couldn't calm down. Usually, I blasted music as I drove. I just rode in silence. A thought entered my mind. I considered driving my car off the road. I thought of killing myself. The thought scared me. I called my mom.

"Please come here," I said. "I'm afraid, Mom. I can't get through this on my own. I need you."

"I will come," she said. "But you can, and you will get through this."

I craved ice cream that night but made a smoothie instead from bananas, cacao nibs, almond milk, and mint. Staving off my craving made me feel stronger and in control. I went through the motions of my skin-care routine, my mind floating somewhere far away. I started with the oil cleanser, gliding the slick vitamin-rich liquid over my skin. It felt like a robot's hand was massaging my face. The foaming cleanser followed, the bubbles popping as I stared blankly into the sink. Toner, essence, serum—I applied each one mechanically. When I reached for the sheet mask package, I vaguely registered its weight in my hand, but the action felt distant and surreal. The mask sat cool and damp against my face, its presence barely grounding me as I drifted further into the blankness, now staring outside the window at the dark night. Eye cream, moisturizer, and essential oil completed the well-rehearsed ritual, my movements slow and deliberate, my mind utterly detached.

The next day, I posted some photos of produce, a stir-fry, a tip for getting a turmeric stain out of plastic, a call to hire a local LA videographer. I tried to seem like I was okay, but I was panicking. I spent much of the day on the phone with my manager.

"At least you haven't been doxed yet," Victoria said.

"What's that?" I asked. I had never heard of it.

"Oh, it happens online a lot," she said. "It's when someone posts your home address or cell phone number online and you get harassed that way. It happened to one of my clients before. A follower posted my client's family's private information, and their house was vandalized overnight."

My mom and dad were still commenting on my posts. Messages like: We love you, Lee. Keep going.

Suddenly, I worried about their safety. I thought of all the times I'd posted photos in their backyard or inside their house. What if someone figured out where they lived from those photos and showed up to their house? I sent a panicked text to my parents and sister:

> Family! I just spoke to my manager who let me know that when one of her clients was bullied, her followers published the family's private information and some fans went to the family house and vandalized it. Probably best not to comment on my photos over the next few days. I'm probably being paranoid, but I want to let you know that this sort of thing happens. I would absolutely be crushed if it did. I know you guys have been so supportive of me and it's so sweet. But it would kill me if this happened.

They texted back that they would quit commenting.

Thirty

I stayed inside the next three days and didn't leave the house. The comments continued.

I heard Lee From America charges $13,000 per post.

I heard she drives an AUDI!

Anyone know her in high school or know her IRL? What's she actually like?

Mommy and daddy prob pay for her apt. it's prob $3,000/month!

A journalist wrote an article explaining the drama. I couldn't imagine what the GOMI Reddit was saying. GOMI was short for Get Off My Internet. It's where trolls and lurkers went to discuss their favorite or most hated people on the internet. It felt like every time I posted, they were alerted to bully me.

Then a sponsor backed out. I was such a fan, the female founder emailed. You go against what most of the wellness industry calls for. You seem to rely on yourself and your intuition the most, which is why it pains me to say that I felt disappointed in the ticket price for your west coast tour this morning. My initial reaction assumed it had to be a major typo. I was about to txt you but as you were explaining in your live, it was not an error. As someone with an event planning background, I understand costs are expensive but there are so many ways this could have been reduced—through sponsors, through event space sponsors, collaborations with locally run stores, so many ways. Especially someone with your platform—there would have been many free options to reduce the price for your followers.

I wasn't sure why this person felt entitled to go off on me with such righteous indignation. Wasn't she a business owner too? Why was everyone so obsessed with me lowering my prices? She was just giving me some of their homemade candles to post. Absurd as it was, it still hurt.

After much deliberation with my team, it was decided that I should be transparent and address the critics. Four days after the initial post, I went onto my stories and said: "Hey guys. I want to address the comments that are saying that my workshop is inaccessible and too expensive for a lot of people. First of all, I understand why people are upset. I apologize if I have personally offended anybody by disabling comments or deleting negativity. My whole goal for this community was to connect with you guys. I give as much as I can while also trying to support myself so I can do this job. As a way to connect with you guys, I realize I've pushed some of you away. I've been so hurt by the comments and my DMs over the last few days. It's made me reconsider this line of work. I know you're not supposed to cry at work, but I always do."

I began crying. After a couple moments, I regained my composure. Then I broke down all my workshop costs: supplies, shipping costs, venue insurance, lodging, flights, all in an effort to be price transparent, a big trend at the time.

In closing, I said: "Let's continue to keep a positive environment where we can support and learn from each other. Let's keep the comments constructive. Negative comments can be very hurtful."

This just made things worse. In the comments I was accused of white tears. Since I posted it as a story rather than to the grid, I was accused of "hiding" it—no matter that I saved it as a highlight. Sharing the cost breakdown of my workshop only invited strangers to give their advice.

> if u did ur workshops at YMCA or the library system, I'm sure u could reduce prices!
>
> Invite 100 people, and charge $100 each. Then you get 10K!

I stopped eating. I stopped going to the gym. I tried to meditate but couldn't. I woke up in the morning with no appetite. I stopped drinking caffeine, not that I needed it. I couldn't sleep. Circles grew under my eyes. My jaw hurt in the morning from grinding my teeth during the few hours I did manage to doze off.

I still did not stop using Instagram. Though I kept my notifications turned off, I posted to stories at least once a day: a recipe, a dance, a monologue about why we shouldn't be self-conscious about dandruff—anything to keep the focus away from the workshops. I wondered if people might see my eye circles and increasing weight loss and understand the hurt I was feeling.

One morning, I got a heart emoji text from Evert's daughter Malin. My heart softened. She wouldn't care about my workshop drama. She just wanted to play on the swings and braid her little sister's hair while telling me about her favorite new dance.

Hi Malin! I texted back. How r u?

It's actually Evert. Call me. Please.

I had blocked him, so he used his daughter's phone to text me. Normally I would have been enraged, but I was so lonely and anxious. I called his number.

"I've seen everything going down," he said. "I want to make sure you are okay."

It was all I wanted. I was so relieved to hear him say it.

"It's been tough," I said. "I mean, I lost my best friend and my business in a week's time."

"You haven't lost your business," Evert said. "You can still recover from this. This is a PR issue. You need to apologize for your reaction. Not for the prices—for the deleted comments. You just need to apologize for upsetting them, then all of this will be over."

I'd upset my followers? What about them upsetting me? Suddenly Evert just sounded like one of my angry fans. I wanted him to shut up and just be on my side, but I suspected he was right.

I called someone I knew who worked closely with musicians, actors, and other entertainers and explained what happened.

"Listen," he said, "this is what happens to every person in the public eye at some point. It's just part of the game. Every celebrity has a scandal. This is yours."

He introduced me to a woman named Sarah who was a PR crisis coach. She helped celebrities craft their public statements and apologies. She usually required a $10,000 retainer, but offered to take me on pro bono.

After reviewing the comments on my recent posts, Sarah said, "These aren't just random trolls. These are your followers who are seriously hurt by your actions."

She confirmed Evert's instincts, advising me to post a more heartfelt video apology to my grid.

The next morning, I got situated in front of my window. I wore no makeup. My hair was pulled back in a loose bun.

"Hi everybody. I wanted to send out an apology for the way that I handled last week's constructive criticism when it came to my workshop tour. I feel very sorry deleting comments, blocking accounts, and disabling entire comment sections. I felt so overwhelmed when those negative comments came in, I got defensive, and my reaction wasn't the best. I apologize. I was never trying to censor anyone or make anyone feel marginalized. I wasn't thinking rationally. This week has been difficult and gut-wrenching. I have wondered if I am cut out for this sort of work. I've doubted myself countless times. I've really been leaning in and reflecting a bunch. I just want to remind you guys that I give all my blog, Instagram, and IG stories away for free. But I need to make a living. Thank you for standing by me as I learn."

I recorded four variations and sent them to Sarah. She picked her favorite, the one in which I looked most vulnerable. She sent me a caption I should include with the post. I read it over and rewatched all four videos. Then I watched them again. And again. The more I watched them, the worse they seemed. I started to look for places I could be criticized. I started to imagine my detractors, what they would say.

I got back in front of the window as the daylight dwindled and recorded three more versions. Each apology was about two minutes.

I sent them to Sarah.

I don't like these as much, she texted. You look uptight, and it sounds like a spiel. More damage control. Look into the camera and talk like it's a friend. Also, keep the camera eye-level, so you're not talking DOWN to your followers.

I recorded one more. The sun was down. My room was dark. My face was dimly lit by a lamp. In the background was a painting a follower had made for me: a rendering of a photo of me sitting in a bathtub that I'd once posted. This time, I held the camera in my hand, not propped up. I didn't need to look at the script. I had memorized it by now. My hair was messier, half up, half down.

I thought it was more authentic than any of the other videos. I sent it to Sarah. As I waited for her to respond, I kept watching the video, over and over, sixteen times. Sarah still hadn't replied.

Hi, I texted her. I felt so uncomfortable bothering her, as I wasn't a paying client. Just checking in . . . how's this one? I think I'm going to post it.

It's good, she texted. Just let the comments come as they will.

Did she really think it was good? Or was she just over me? Whatever the case, I didn't want to delay longer. I posted[24] it on my feed.

Comments poured in—ultimately more than two thousand.

Corey commented, called and texted multiple times to make sure you were okay, but you never hit me back. Because Corey had a blue check mark, it shot to the top. Drama ensued.

> why didn't she text u back? Bizarre she hasn't reached out.

> @corey want to know more . . does she always ignore u?

The trolls didn't stop with me. They also found Dalen and started flooding her comments. She pushed back, responding sharply to each and every one. I encouraged her to stop.

"Dalen, I really think these commenters have something real and honest to say," I said. "That we, that I, need to look at our privilege."

"My brother is in prison," she said. "Nobody knows that. He has tattoos all over his body. All over. The justice system is so fucked. He's been in there for a decade. He killed a man. Accidentally. But he's a changed man now, and they still have him locked up. He even talks differently now."

I wasn't sure how that was related to what we were experiencing. I just thanked her for sharing.

Thirty-One

I was sensitive now to everything. I went to dinner with a few restaurant owners in town from New York City, and when I got back into my car, I saw that my last selfie had only received twenty-five thousand likes in three hours. I was crushed and drove back to my apartment feeling like a failure.

You suck.

Nobody likes you anymore.

You're over.

you are irrelevant.

I started to actually consider, for the first time, that maybe I wasn't tough enough for this job. I didn't have it in me to constantly reinvent, innovate, and renew. I wasn't comfortable being just average either. If I was going to be an influencer, I needed to be the best. I was starting to notice that social justice influencers were having their moment. Did I need to pivot to those kinds of posts?

My anxiety increased even more when I got an email that an episode of a popular beauty/wellness podcast I'd guested on was now up. I turned it on while driving on the 405, and within ten minutes, I began panicking. The hosts and I were talking about Grimes and Elon Musk, who'd begun dating earlier that year and debuted their relationship at the Met Gala.

"She's so skinny," a host said.

"She's like all knees," I said.

And then I did an impersonation of her singing her big banger, "Genesis."

The episode had been recorded two weeks after my cancelation. I'd shown up to their dark rented studio in Burbank gripping my Hydro Flask full of black chaga tea and bracing for an awkward conversation—but the hosts, hilarious and unhinged in the best way, immediately put me at ease. These girls were not perfectionists, and they weren't trying to be, so I could let myself be less than a perfect girlboss. I forgot about having to be Lee From America and just let loose.

Now, when I heard myself talking about Grimes, I worried it sounded like I was being mean-spirited and body-shaming. Trained to view myself through the lens of my online haters, I was terrified that I would be accused of bringing another woman down.

I took my foot off the gas, pulled to the side of the highway, and frantically called my manager. "Victoria, we need, I repeat, we *need* to get this taken down. *Now.* Aren't they supposed to send it to us first for approval?"

"Sometimes podcasts do that," she said. "Other times, they don't. It's not that bad. I listened to the whole thing, and it sounded—"

"No, it needs to be taken down."

"Okay," she said. "Let me talk to them."

Back at my apartment, I opened my email to see a back-and-forth between my team and the podcast. They really did not want to remove it, but once we copied my lawyer on the email, they acquiesced.

"That can't happen again," Victoria said. "It's nice that they removed it. Anything you say on the air you must assume is going to be released. Let this be a learning lesson for you."

I felt calm for a moment. Then, I worried that I'd burned that bridge and ruined my relationship with the hosts of the podcast.

Given my anxiety, I didn't know how I was going to withstand the scrutiny of doing the workshops. But I knew canceling them would cost me the respect of many of the followers I still had. And I worried about losing more brand partnerships and job opportunities; I couldn't afford not to take the work and bank some money.

Prior to scheduling the workshops, I asked an Ayurvedic woman of Indian descent if she'd be okay with me teaching some of the things she taught me in her book. I would credit her, of course. She said absolutely, but I was terrified I'd be called out for cultural appropriation. I was also terrified that if I didn't include her teachings, she'd call me out for promising her I'd share her lessons to others and then reneging. I know now she would have never done such a thing. She was so incredibly kind. But that's how spun out and paranoid I was.

I decided to keep it in.

The workshops themselves went well. There were moments when I forgot what had happened, when it felt like everything was normal and that I was still the happy-go-lucky influencer these followers had been admiring for years. But after the workshops I'd have a Q&A, and someone always brought up the cancelation, even in an oblique way. At the Seattle workshop, someone asked: "How do you handle all the negativity?"

Silence fell over the room. It always did during these Q&As when this kind of question was asked. Everybody who showed up was still a fan of mine. But they were also curious to know how I was holding up.

I'm scared and ready to go into a cave and hide forever.

That was the honest answer. Instead I said the same thing I always did.

"I'm okay. It's been hard, but I'm okay."

Another girl shot her hand up.

"Can you tell us about white privilege?" she asked.

It was the first time I'd gotten this question on the tour, but I was prepared.

"I'm not really in a position to do that, as a white person," I said.

I'd read that this was the appropriate response to such a question.

That night, the last of the tour, there was a VIP dinner for those attendees who wanted an extra special experience. One of them said to me, "I noticed you've been storying less."

It didn't matter what I said to my followers. They were onto me. They could tell from my decreased posting how I'd been affected. And so I decided to be honest for a change.

"It's been hard," I said. "I've been doubting myself a ton."

The girl nodded, and the table fell silent. I watched as my VIP followers looked down at their plates, cutting into their charred roasted vegetables and rotisserie chicken. In my increasing paranoia, I worried they would think I was trying to play the victim. That one of them would leave the dinner and post about how I couldn't handle criticism about my privilege, or that my apology was just for damage control and I didn't mean any of it. I understand now that their silent nodding was a kindness, a gentle acknowledgment of what I'd said— but there was no reasoning with my brain at that point.

Thirty-Two

My behavior started getting more erratic and obsessive. My approach to food started to increasingly resemble how it'd been in high school.

I was sent to Japan by a new travel app. I could bring a guest, so my mom came along.

"I'm just preparing you," I said to her on the plane. "You're going to have to take lots of photos of me on this trip."

She took pictures of me on the street, at a shrine, in a mall. When we weren't taking photos, I was on my phone, endlessly searching for healthy versions of Japan's most popular dishes. I spent four hours trying to find us a soba shop that served gluten-free noodles. I wasn't even celiac. I just thought they were healthier.

There was a lot of smoking in Japan. I always wanted to smoke when I was starving myself. I couldn't with my mom there, so I would stand close to smokers, trying to get a whiff.

On our second morning in Tokyo, I was still jet-lagged and woke up at 5:45. I crept out of our hotel room, careful not to wake my mom. I walked the dark, silent streets and grabbed a black coffee from the first vending machine I saw. First, I double-checked the caloric content to make sure there was no sugar added. I pulled up Google Maps and decided to walk three miles to a shrine at the edge of Tokyo. By the time I got back to the hotel, I'd have walked six miles and it'd only be 8:30. Then I could do a full day of sightseeing on foot, getting my steps up to thirty thousand—or thirteen miles—in a day. I always loved traveling for the number of steps it was socially acceptable to take. Nobody could say I was overexercising or falling back into old habits here.

When I returned to the hotel, my mom was just waking up. When she asked where I'd gone, I told her I'd just taken a short walk around the block. For breakfast, I was just going to have an apple from the big bowl of fruit the hotel had arranged in our room. But there were only red apples. I started to panic. The hormonal protocol I'd been following said to only eat green apples. Red ones could spike my blood sugar. I couldn't do that.

"Hey, Mom, do we have any green apples?" I asked.

"I think that's all the apples we've got," she called from the bathroom.

I was starting to feel dizzy and empty, the familiar feeling of being too hungry, which could lead to a binge later in the day.

My mom came out of the bathroom, smiling at the thought of all the sightseeing she'd planned for us to do that day.

"I thought we'd go to the fish market today—"

"No!" I shouted. "It needs to be green!"

Her smile disappeared. She immediately knew that there was no rationalizing with me or calming me down. Our day wouldn't begin until we found a green apple.

The fruit stand down the street didn't have one. We took the subway to another neighborhood and started hunting for fruit stalls. My entire mind was overtaken with a determination to find this green apple. With each block, I became more and more anxious, more and more rigid and inflexible about this green apple. I was fixated on this apple. It was the only food that felt safe to eat. Even though I was in Japan with some of the best food in the world, I was determined to find an apple and would not budge.

Finally, we found one.

Relaxation swept over me.

"Okay, now what?" I said casually as I chewed, as if it was no big deal I'd just wasted hours on this distressing quest. My mom looked exasperated.

I'd done a lot of reading about culture in Japan. Apparently slurping was not considered rude. It was actually a compliment to the chef.

While eating vegan ramen one night, I storied myself slurping noodles. Immediately, I got a DM.

> This is so racist of you. Please do not mock the slurping as a white woman.

I panicked and deleted the story, the familiar feeling of am-I-going-to-get-canceled washing over me. I felt like I couldn't get anything right. I realize now I was starting to disassociate. I did not feel present. I did not feel safe. I defaulted to the only thing I knew to do to give myself meaning and remind myself that I existed. I posted. I went on a posting spree. Any amount of validation would momentarily ease the noise in my head. I constantly asked my mom to take photos[25] of me: standing in the middle of street intersections, browsing in malls, praying at shrines. One night in the hotel, missing Evert, I danced around to Amy Winehouse's "Valerie," a song about getting back together with an old lover. In the video, I am bouncing around in a miniskirt and no bra, my boobs much smaller now from all the stress and low appetite.

I posted the video and comments poured in.

OMG 🔥🔥🔥

You look great!!!!!

What's your diet and exercise regime?

I took these comments as a sign that I was healthy. My mind relaxed. Then I panicked. Would I always have to be in so much pain to be praised?

Thirty-Three

Returning from the Japan trip didn't curb my growing mania. In the Uber back from the airport, I made the driver stop so I could buy an espresso machine. I decided I was sick of matcha. But I would only make myself americanos and espresso, too afraid to drink lattes, which contained a lot of milk.

On a similar whim, I decided to get a puppy. One Saturday, I woke up at six a.m. to drive to Orange County to attend a large pet adoption event. Of course, I made sure to film it. "I feel like I'm about to become a new parent," I said to the camera. "I'm so nervous I couldn't sleep all night. But it feels so right. I hope I find the one."

I walked around the event and spotted a sandy-colored mixed-breed with Lab ears. His name was Rascal. When I picked him up, he peed on me. I put him back down and kept walking.

Next, I came across a white dog with a black spot on its ear. I held him in my arms. He wasn't it either. I put him down.

Looking for a dog became like me looking for a green apple. I had to have the right one. I wasn't sure what the right one would be. But I was sure that I would know it when I found it.

After a couple laps around the space, I approached a pen with eight husky-looking puppies, all rolling around and playing with each other. One stood out: sand-colored with a white chest, dark snout, big droopy brown eyes, one ear pointing straight up and the other flopping over. I watched him wrestle with the others for a few minutes. He was the most beautiful dog I'd ever seen.

The woman tending the puppies said his name was Samson. He was eight weeks old and this was his first time outside. I picked him up and held him to my chest, his whole body relaxing. He looked at me with his big eyes and snuggled up to my neck.

Here was my green apple.

I started filling out the paperwork but suddenly got nervous. Obsessiveness began to take hold. He might've been a green apple, but was he the *best* green apple? Maybe there was another dog here that was an even better fit for me. I put him back in the pen and told the woman I just wanted to do one more lap.

What was I looking for? I wasn't sure. But my path through the space started to slow as the event got more crowded. I started to panic. What if someone else had found Samson? What if they were signing the paperwork right now? I hurried back to his pen, lightly pushing through the crowd. When I got to his pen, it was just as I'd worried. A dozen people were gathered around, some pointing to Samson. I tried to get the attention of the woman, but another man was talking to her.

"I want Samson!" I yelled loudly. "Please! Please! I'll sign the papers!"

The woman gave me a distressed look, wondering why I was making such a scene.

"Don't worry," she said. "He's yours."

After I signed the papers and Venmoed her $250, she put him in my arms, and I carried him toward my car. People stared at us, oohing and aahing as I walked past. I was ecstatic. But as we got farther from the crowd, I realized how unprepared I was. I didn't have food for him back home, or a bed. I didn't even have a leash.

I stopped at a bench and sat down. I needed to collect myself. Tears began streaming down my face as I held his little body. I felt his arms wrapping around my biceps. He was scared.

"I'll protect you," I said to him. "It's okay."

I began to sob. Then I pulled out my phone and recorded the moment: me weeping as Samson chewed grass at my feet.

I decided not to post it. I wanted to introduce Samson to my followers with a post that used the same kind of artful staging as my smoothie bowls. When we got back to the apartment, after a stop at Petco for supplies, I set him up for a photo shoot. Though I hadn't picked him because he went with my apartment's aesthetic, he absolutely did, his taupe color blending perfectly with my cream-colored furniture and bedding. The post[26] got sixty thousand likes—my most liked photo yet.

I understand now that while adopting a dog on a total whim was an example of my declining mental health, that wasn't all it was. I was craving some kind of connection with real life—something that wasn't filtered and fake from the refraction of social media. I needed something to ground me, a tether to the real world. And over the coming years, he would fill me with so much love and so much comfort. But I now understand that posting that first photo and seeing how many likes it got distorted how I viewed him. It apportioned an algorithmic value to him. I had turned him into another prop—like everything else in my life.

Thirty-Four

The main @instagram account featured me on their page. They wanted to promote @leefromamerica as a health and wellness account that spoke with authenticity and promoted self-care. Unfortunately, the photo they'd featured was the one of me holding illegally obtained California poppies. It drew some negative comments, but within a week I had thirty thousand new followers. I couldn't let such an opportunity go to waste. I wanted to impress them, entice them. I pushed new content hard. It was that old feeling: You're getting a lot of eyeballs on you, you need to perform.

    The stress was mounting as Samson disrupted my strict routine. Every morning, I carried him down my apartment stairs to the back corner of my building's private turf puppy park that nobody else used. Early puppyhood meant he had to go down first thing in the morning and usually five more times a day. I could no longer wake up and meditate or go to the gym. I was mostly stuck at home. Errands like going to the grocery store or picking up grooming products were infrequent, since brands were sending me so much stuff. In my mounting claustrophobia, I followed my moon journal and tried to practice a full-moon ritual for the Gemini placement, which called for a variety of herbs, twigs, and rocks. But I didn't have time to pick up all the ingredients. So this ritual that was meant to calm my anxiety just increased it.

I realized I needed some help, and booked an appointment with a therapist. The therapist's office was attached to her beautiful Beverly Hills home.

"I feel very isolated," I told her. "I'm having trouble with food. I'm not wanting to eat, and when I do eat, at the slightest sensation of fullness, I panic. I'm leaning back into restrictive tendencies I had as a teenager."

"Simple," the therapist said. "Just eat."

I couldn't believe she was giving me this advice. I spent the rest of the session in a daze. Driving home, I stuck the car's stress-reduction aromatherapy diffuser an inch up my nose, even though the warning label states to never do that. I inhaled it deeply through one nostril, then the other. The scent of lavender, chamomile, and jasmine was the only thing keeping me together.

The gulf between online life and real life continued to widen. My sponsorships had rebounded since the cancelation. I was hired to work with a water bottle brand, posting a special edition bottle I illustrated and designed. And I was invited to Palm Springs to post[27] about a flea market for artisans who made things like soy-free scented candles and hand-dyed indigo underwear. They put me and Samson up for the weekend in the $500-a-night Ace Hotel. But sitting on a bench outside my room and walking the grounds, I smoked from a pack of American Spirits I had picked up at a nearby gas station. Normally, I would have never smoked in public around people, afraid that one of my followers might see me and expose me for such unhealthy behavior that contradicted my brand. But I didn't care. I almost hoped I'd be caught, so that my entire career and all its toxicity would come crumbling down.

On Instagram, I was immersed in an often cruel world that I could neither control nor predict. Every time I opened the app, I saw a comment that would send me into a space of numbness and panic. Every nerve in my body screamed for me to retreat further, to find solace in the shadows of my own space. My isolation and solitude increased.

For the first time in my life, I didn't spend Christmas in Connecticut with my family. I told them it was because I was burned out from traveling and couldn't travel with my new puppy. With the workshops and various jobs, I'd taken nearly thirty flights that year. But really it was just me continuing to withdraw from life. On Christmas Eve, I wrote in my journal, *I feel scared by my hunger. I have a distorted view of the world right now. I do not feel happy. I feel suicidal. I want to smoke cigarettes. I feel like destructing.*

On New Year's Eve, I walked from my apartment in Koreatown to Little Tokyo to pick up dinner: four pieces of sashimi, four wedges of sweet potato. I photographed it and posted it on my finsta with the caption Happy New Year!

Instantly, I received a message from a friend: That's all you're having?

In my deluded state, I took it as a compliment rather than a criticism.

Eventually, my mental deterioration started to impact my work.

I was hired to do a sponsored set of stories for a healthy dog food brand. Now that I had Samson, I was getting inundated with new opportunities for dog-related products. I'd already recorded the videos and they'd been approved. But for some reason, when the scheduled time to post came, I couldn't do it. A few minutes passed, then a half hour, then an hour, then three. I was getting continuous texts from my manager.

Hey Lee! The brand wants to know when
you plan on posting the stories?

Hey Lee, we gotta post today.

She called, but I wouldn't answer. I curled up in a ball on my rug, my heart pounding. I couldn't bear to open the Instagram app. I finally uploaded the stories just so my manager's calls and texts would stop. I felt such a deep self-loathing and disconnect from the character I was forced to portray online: a healthy, happy Lee with a bright smile and all the products she could ever want. I didn't wait to see how the stories performed. I just quickly closed the app and stayed on the floor for another hour, Samson coming over every now and then to sniff my face.

I realized I needed to find a new manager—one who was more sympathetic to the crisis I was in, so I started interviewing new ones. I told them I was thinking of taking a little break to focus on my mental health.

"How long of a break are you thinking?" one of them said.

"I'm not sure," I said. "Maybe one to three months?"

There was a pause.

"Well," he said, "I think a hiatus would be *totally* on brand for you. You could then turn the break into a series of videos about lessons you learned, and maybe we could find a corporate sponsor for your official comeback."

Thirty-Five

That January, it rained hard, as it often did that time of year in LA. On a third consecutive day of rain, I returned home from an errand and found water pouring from the ceiling. There were three inches of water on the floor. Samson sat in his crate, completely soaked and shivering. The light fixtures were filled with brown water. My laptop was drenched. Everything was—the entire apartment, everything in it, every perfectly Instagramable corner, was sopping wet. The cookbooks and health books. The trinkets from Etsy. The Urban Outfitters ottoman. The dozens of Outdoor Voices workout sets. The Floyd desk. Years and years of stuff I'd been sent. What was it all worth, I wondered. Over $100,000 easily.

I began to sob. Then the question occurred to me another way.

What was it all worth?

The rug, the daybed, the throw pillows, the bed pillows, the bed frame, the sheets, the mattress, the nightstand, the books on the nightstand, the books on the bookshelf, the bookshelf, the bathroom vanity full of face masks and cleansers and serums and even the toothbrush: everything I owned had all been gifted to me. I hadn't bought any of it with money I'd earned. I hadn't acquired any of it because I saw it and thought, *That's how I see myself and how I want to communicate my vision of myself with the world.* None of it was an act of self-expression. None of it represented my personal aesthetic. I had no idea what my personal aesthetic was. These were all props I'd been using, like an actor on a Broadway stage. But for me, the play was never over. It had been running practically twenty-four hours a day, seven days a week, for years. Now I realized it wasn't just all this stuff that was props. I was a prop too—a disposable, soulless, increasingly emaciated mannequin used by companies to sell more stuff. We all were—all the billions of us who thought we were using Instagram when really it was the other way around. I post a photo wearing a matching tank-top-and-leggings set. Someone sees that and buys the same set and posts a photo of themselves in it. Someone else sees that and buys it and posts a photo of themselves in it. Someone else sees that and buys it and posts a photo of themselves in it. Someone else sees that and buys it and posts a photo of themselves in it. Don't forget to hashtag. Don't forget to tag. Short captions drive more engagement. Long captions drive more engagement. Commenting on comments drives more engagement. Driving more engagement is lame. Posting to the grid is lame. Posting to the grid is cool. Post the thirst trap. Slide into the DMs. Deep like accidentally. Deep like intentionally. Soft launch the relationship. Unfollow after the breakup. Delete the soft launch post or leave it up? Definitely delete it, right? Look at that ring. Look at that wedding. Look at those kids. What's wrong with that kid? Why are his teeth like that? Why is she posting photos of her kids? Wait, did they get divorced? Why did she stop posting photos of her husband? What's her problem? Why hasn't she talked about it? Why is she being so secretive? Why is she still talking about it? Why hasn't she moved on already? I miss you, Grandma. You were taken too soon, Mom. I wish you were still here, Dad. Best dad ever. Best brunch ever. Best workout ever. Thanks @leefromamerica for the outfit rec and discount code.

So: What *was* it all worth?

Not much.

Rather than be devastated by this—that the last few years of my life weren't life at all but just one big bullshit advertising campaign—I felt liberated, finally wide awake for the first time in my adult life. I grabbed Samson, my destroyed laptop, soggy passport, and got into my car. I wasn't sure where I was going, but wherever it was would at least be real.

For the next few weeks, I bounced around from place to place, crashing with friends and staying at Airbnbs. Eventually, I found a studio to sublet in Highland Park. The musician who lived there was going on tour. It was one room. The windows opened to an alley. No sunrise views. No direct sunlight even. No antique brass doorknobs, just the metal hospital kind. It was not Instagram-friendly. It was perfect.

I had retrieved some of my things from the old apartment that weren't too damaged from the flood. But most of it I put out on the street in front of my new place. As I was setting down the Le Creuset dishware and Urban Outfitters wicker furniture, a woman walked by.

"This is all free?" she asked.

"Yes," I said.

She got on her knees.

"I prayed to God today that He would answer my prayers, and look what the Lord delivered! Thank you, Lord Jesus, and thank you, kind woman!"

I sat in the screened-in vestibule for much of the afternoon, watching people stop by and take my things, one by one: my framed art prints, my kitchen appliances, my leggings, my shoes. It was cathartic to watch everything I'd accumulated disappear.

Thirty-Six

I texted the woman with the pink hair I'd met at the Silver Lake recovery meeting nearly four years earlier. I'd had her number saved in my phone that whole time, but this was the first time I used it.

> Fiona, it's Lee. I hope this finds you well. We met back in 2015 or so. I just wanted to ask to see what your favorite meetings are.

She called me immediately and gave me some recommendations. I wasn't sure if I had a drinking problem, but I realized the impulse to drink and drug like I did earlier in my twenties didn't just disappear, it shifted. The obsession, the identity, the personality, the escape, it had just found a new home in health. And it could easily shift back into drugs, and I feared that this time I wouldn't reach for coke or molly, but something even worse. A few weeks of meetings made me realize how crippling my anxiety was. And the biggest culprit, without question, was social media.

One morning, I recorded a video and posted it on stories. I only did one take, even though I was annoyed by the sound of my voice. As soon as I hit record, I always instinctively defaulted to my Instagram voice: higher, perkier, annunciated, almost screaming.

"Hi, everybody. I am going to be taking off some extended time from Instagram. I'm going to be back for sure, but right now I need to turn inward and not use social media. I've been using this platform for five years, and I've never taken off more than ten days. Not that I even need to justify it. I've been talking myself out of it because of fear. This is a challenge for me. I'm excited to see what happens. I'm excited to go through the motions of life without using social media. I love you guys and I'm looking forward to returning. In the meantime, mwah!" I blew a kiss.

The DMs poured in, and people starting commenting on my last grid photo. No wonder she is leaving, someone wrote. You guys are horrible to her.

The last DM I read said, Good luck with your hiatus babe! You deserve it..but before u leave, where is ur necklace from again?

I resisted the compulsion to keep reading. I closed the app and deleted it from my phone.[28]

Thirty-Seven

My sublet was ending soon, and I decided my first act of embracing life without social media would be buying a house. I had been renting since college, and I wanted a place that was truly mine—something I could design and decorate the way I actually wanted to. Part of the desire, I admit, was that achieving homeownership by the age of thirty would signal success to my parents, who had never quite taken my career as an influencer as seriously as, say, a job in "stable" corporate America. I found a real estate agent, got preapproved for a mortgage, and started looking.

I also decided to see a therapist who specialized in disordered eating—one who wouldn't just tell me to "eat more." After our initial consultation, the therapist spoke to me candidly.

"By the sound of your symptoms, I think you might benefit from more intensive treatment. Have you thought about checking out a center?"

The thought of going to a full-blown treatment center seemed like overkill. It felt like I was regressing, like I was back to being that kid in high school who had to go to Florida. But I decided I'd at least get some more information before I made a decision.

The center I visited was in Beverly Hills on the top floor of a bank. I took the elevator with a bunch of people in suits and ties heading to their office jobs. By the casual way I was dressed, I was sure they knew where I was headed. I wore red high-waisted sailor pants, a white shirt, and bright orange Fenty coral lipstick. The lipstick was one of the few gifted items I had kept from the flood. I mean, it was Fenty, and the shade looked great on me.

I sat in the waiting room and filled out a form, then sat some more until my name was called. There were no magazines in the waiting room, and from my time at the Florida treatment center, I knew why: They were often too triggering with their idealized body standards and diet regimens. Rotating on a flat screen were photos of activities and events at the center, including a girl my age painting by a window.

The door finally opened. A middle-aged woman with short, straight brown hair with blonde highlights poked her head out.

"Lee?"

I stood up and followed her khaki capris and tiny ballet flats to her office. Looking at her feet, I notice she had a tattoo of a phrase I'd heard a few times in the meetings I'd been going to: *Right now, it's like this*.

A pink sign next to her office door read TO DREAM IT IS TO BE IT. Inside, a large window overlooked West Los Angeles. Diplomas hung on the wall behind the desk. On the desk was a small fake succulent. It was always easy to spot the fake ones. They were too green, too shiny. Even though I was taking a break from social media, I couldn't help scouting any room I walked into for good photo setups.

The woman's name was Laurel. She was the director of the center. She sat behind her desk, and I took a seat at one of the two chairs in front of it.

"So?" she said.

"So," I said.

"What brings you in today, Lee?"

"I had an eating disorder when I was sixteen. Then I went to treatment. And I think I just need a brushup on recovery. I'm a health and wellness blogger, you see. Well, I was. I'm on hiatus now. I'm thinking about food all the time. I'm afraid of my hunger. I hate it. I question it. I don't trust it. I'm terrified of gaining weight. I can't really go out to dinner with friends—not that I have many."

Laurel nodded and listened.

"And if I can't exercise, I panic. And I take a lot of pics of my body to measure it since I don't let myself use a scale."

The words poured out of me. It was like a confession. I wondered if I should tell her I was afraid of Clorox, bleach, ammonia, and most chemicals. I decided not to and to stick only to food. I told her a bit more—including the story of searching for the green apple and how the other night I'd eaten two paleo vanilla bars and nearly a whole tub of cashew yogurt with paleo granola, then tried on all my pants, frantic to see if I'd gained weight. I even took photos of myself in various positions, lifting my shirt.

"Thank you for sharing all that," Laurel said. "Have you heard of the term orthorexia?"

"Yes," I said, remembering when Evert gave me articles about it.

"Oftentimes, patients convolute healthy eating patterns with dieting, especially if they have a history of disordered eating and dieting."

I nodded.

"I think you could seriously benefit from day treatment here. It's a six-week program, Monday through Friday, 8:30 a.m. to 2:30 p.m. You'd have breakfast and lunch with us, group and individual therapy, nutrition therapy, a psychiatric evaluation, psychoeducation, group exercise, and art therapy."

"Um," I said, "that sounds a little intense. I thought I'd just do some sort of group, like, you know, a few times a month."

Laurel smiled. "I know what you mean. I'm just sharing my two cents on where you're at. I believe you are a little far gone for just supplemental group therapy. I really think you could benefit from intensive day treatment."

"Uh-huh," I said. And then it hit me.

I didn't eat gluten, soy, or dairy. Yet I had no food allergies.

I only ate organic.

I was afraid of plastic.

I was afraid of gaining weight.

I was afraid of what would happen to my body if I stopped exercising. Skipping an exercise class made me anxious.

I wore an Apple Watch to track my calories, steps, and movement.

I wouldn't eat at certain restaurants.

I often needed to be in control of when, how, and what I ate when going out with groups.

I was always thinking about food.

And I skipped meals.

"I understand this may be a lot to take in," Laurel said. "Feel free to take a few days to think about it. In the meantime, we can go ahead and call your insurance to see what your coverage is."

I agreed and drove home. Later that afternoon, the center called. My insurance would not cover the treatment. They didn't even offer a partial reimbursement. If I decided to do this, I would need to pay completely out of pocket.

I opened my new laptop and logged in to my bank. The facility would cost me the same amount as a down payment on a house. I couldn't afford both. I'd have to pick.

I called Fiona, who I was now talking to regularly. I told her my dilemma and asked what she thought I should do. She was silent for a moment.

"Lee," she said, "if you buy the house with the money instead of investing in your health, you'll lose the house anyway."

It wasn't what I wanted to hear, but it was exactly what I needed to hear. I knew she was right. I started the treatment program the following week.

Epilogue

My girlfriends sitting at the Hugo's Tacos picnic table looked at me, barely blinking, blowing clouds of fruit-flavored vape smoke into the air above us. I didn't have to tell them the rest of the story.

They knew how hard it'd been that first morning of treatment for me to eat Cheerios with whole milk instead of almond milk—to eat Cheerios at all rather than matcha for breakfast.

They knew about the weigh-ins, how unlike other treatment facilities, ours believed it was helpful for patients to know their weight and be accepting of it. They knew how I had a number in my head that terrified me and that on the day I surpassed it, I put my head in my hands and cried—but then completely forgot about the number a few hours later. They knew about my fear of fluoride, and how shortly after abandoning it I developed six cavities.

They knew how I took six magnesium pills a day because I thought it helped with constipation, and how one of my homework assignments was to throw them away along with all my powders: Dream Blend, Focus Root, and Moon Mend, which I chucked so hard into the large construction dumpster they broke, the brown and pearlescent powders flying everywhere.

They knew how one of my other homework assignments was a trip to Ralph's, the first time in years I'd gone to a grocery store that wasn't Whole Foods or Erewhon, and how I had a panic attack and ran out, but then went back a week later and grabbed non-organic milk, regular tomatoes, bacon, mayonnaise, white bread, Goldfish, Lucky Charms, and turkey slices from the deli—not free-range or organic, just regular old turkey slices, the ones with preservatives.

They knew all this because I'd met them at the treatment center. They were going through the same thing, and we discussed it all in group therapy, during hangouts near the center, and in the months that followed. For first time since high school, I had a circle of friends. We started a group chat and would send each other funny memes about recovery. We had picnics in Elysian Park with our dogs. We played board games. We did clothing swaps.

"Wow, what's this brand?" they'd ask.

"Reformation," I'd say.

"What's that?"

These girls were normal. They were not living their lives online. Everything I'd told them about my former life as an influencer was all the more surprising to them. They were a little surprised that I hadn't felt I could share it with them. But they understood I wanted to start fresh and put all that in the past.

"I still don't understand how you can go from doing drugs and partying in New York to drinking matcha and doing yoga in LA," Jordan said.

"Extreme wellness is all about control," I said. "So for people who are feeling out of control and partying a lot, the lifestyle shift to wellness is very attractive. The harder you hoe, the harder you heal. If there's a girl online posting about sunsets and rainbows, you better believe she has seen some shit."

"Do you think you'll ever go back on Instagram?" one of them asked.

"Well," I said, "I use my finsta, which you guys know about, which is just for friends and family. But yes, I do think I will. It was never my intention to stay off permanently. I don't think that's realistic. Sometimes I wish we lived in a world where social media didn't exist. But it does, and there's no going back to the way things were, much as we might try. And so I don't think it makes sense to totally abstain from it. To me, that also seems like living an illusion—a different kind of illusion than living entirely online, but still an illusion."

That's how I continue to feel today. I've since resumed posting on Instagram as @leefromamerica. And after moving back to the East Coast with Samson and spending some time working as a social media director for a tech company, I'm now open to making money from my own social media again—and I've even hosted workshops to help influencers use their skills to explore other career paths.

Some people in my comments have called me a hypocrite for these workshops. So she's influencing people against influencing? I understand the criticism. It took me a long time to realize my relationship with my work online required a nuanced approach—not all or nothing. When I quit influencing, I was against making money at all, ranting to anyone who would listen how I refused to participate in "late-stage capitalism." I had little idea what that term actually meant but I loved how righteous I sounded when I said it. I quickly realized that it wasn't righteous, it was privileged and unrealistic, and that such virtue isn't so easy to maintain when there's rent to pay and groceries to buy, and that no matter how much I complained, nobody was going to take care of me but me, and that money allows me to experience the world and follow my passions, and that I have to support myself however I can.

I know I'm not saying anything here that a lot of people don't already know—especially younger people. According to a survey I saw recently, more than half of Gen Z wants to pursue social media influencing as a career. As far as jobs go, it can be a pretty good one. I'm not denying that.

So long as it stays a job. So long as it doesn't blur the line between professional and personal so much that you jeopardize your sanity. I'm not against influencing as a career. What I'm against is not being aware of the dangers and completely losing yourself online the way I did and forgetting all the joy and beauty of the real world. Finding that balance isn't easy when using a technology that was designed to be addictive, but I feel that given my experience, I'm perfectly positioned to help people try.

That night at the taco place was a step toward finding that balance for myself.

"Well, if you're going to be on it," said Mackenzie, "you shouldn't be one of those creeps who just looks at people's posts without posting anything yourself. Here, let me take a photo of you."

She grabbed my phone and snapped a pic—just one—then handed it right back. I looked at the photo. It was the first time I'd seen a photo of myself in months. Back when I first started my hiatus, even though I wasn't posting, I still couldn't quit the habit of taking selfies. I'd take hundreds a day—in front of my mirror, in the car (seatbelt on), outside the treatment center building. It was a reflex. But it felt more weird and ridiculous as the weeks went on. I did it less and less until I wasn't doing it at all.

Looking at the photo, I was surprised by what I saw. It wasn't like I hadn't seen myself in a mirror. But seeing a photo was different, especially since for so many years, that was how I measured my worth.

Halfway through my time at the treatment center, I went to a Silver Lake salon and asked the stylist for a bowl cut. "Like the kind Jim Carrey had in *Dumb and Dumber*," I told her. She smirked and chuckled, thinking I was being sarcastic. "No, I'm serious," I said. "Give me the full Carrey." I wanted a clean slate, and I thought it would help further rid me of my impulses toward idealized beauty standards. Also, if I looked like a weirdo, maybe I'd be less inclined to take selfies. Afterward, when I FaceTimed my mom and dad, they freaked out—which meant the stylist totally nailed it.

It had grown out a bit since then and was looking less bizarre—clearly, given the follower who'd recognized me in the taco line. Still, as I looked at the photo, I started laughing. Because for the first time in a long time, I recognized the person in it. I was smiling because I was with people I enjoyed and we were having a good time. I was wearing clothes of theirs I'd gotten in one of our swaps—blue overalls and a green hoodie that I'd pulled up to stay warm as the Los Angeles night turned brisk. They were comfortable clothes, clothes that I had been drawn to and that conveyed a newfound self-acceptance. I looked goofy. I looked happy. I looked like myself.[29]

I hit post, then put my phone away and enjoyed the rest of the night with my friends.

Acknowledgments

First and foremost, thank you to my family for loving me fearlessly throughout all my phases: Mom, Dad, Lexie, Peter, and Jack. I love you guys. Aunt Didi, for always seeing me as a writer, not just a blogger. My cousin Laura. My grandmother Tilly, for being such a beautiful presence in my life and always cheering on my creative endeavors. I have a ninety-four-year-old grandmother who reads my newsletter. How lucky I am to have such a strong family.

I want to thank my friends and my IRL community who held my hand throughout this wild process of stepping away from the internet and coming back to share my story. Voice memos, texts, calls out of the blue, check-ins, coffee dates, cards, notes, and hugs—I felt your presence even when we were apart: AJ Marechal, Emma Grady, Caitlin Confort, Skidoo, Adam Himebauch, Isolde Walters, Lucy Biggers, Jess Elefante, Margaret Cissel, Jess Defino, Kate Lindsay, Becca B., Rhiannon, Liza Kraft, Laura Whitmore, Catie Horseman, Clare Kutsko, Lina Abascal, Sarah Levy, Adam Krasner, Sidney Bird, Paula Mannis, Sadie Adams, Bennett Konesni, Jess Griffiths, Alex Hollender, Annah Kessler, Emma Riley, Margaret May, Anne, Joss, Morgan, Sunshine, and Skandia.

Places are just as meaningful as people, so I want to thank the town of Ojai for your endless beauty. You've always been a place for me to land and come back to myself. I wrote much of this book in Ojai, and, while there, met some of the kindest people I've ever encountered. To the staff of the Dutchess, specifically, thank you for the delicious coffee and for providing your town with such a welcoming place to work, eat, and be with their neighbors.

Thank you to Sylvester Manor and the farmhands I had the privilege of working alongside during that unforgettable summer of 2009. You played a pivotal role in unearthing my connection to food and intentional living before it was cool.

Thank you to my English teachers at SJU: Aimée Knight, in whose class I wrote my senior thesis on humblebragging and social media—a seed that, in many ways, grew into this very work—and Tom Coyne, who believed in me relentlessly.

Thank you to the NYPL Rose Reading Room, the Center for Fiction and its incredible writers and staff, and the countless six a.m. Zoom writers' groups I joined when this book was still just an idea. Every bit of feedback, support, presence, and camaraderie helped carry it forward.

And, of course—thank you to my team who helped bring this book to life, especially my agent, Lauren, who believed in it the most and always kept me grounded.

And to Simon & Schuster, specifically Sean Manning, thank you for tending to the vision, helping me cut through the fluff, and for seeing the story below the story. Thank you for protecting the integrity of my experience, even when I cringed. You've changed how I view writing forever.

Thank you to those who supported my healing through the years: Heather and Beth at Renfrew, the entire staff at Fairwinds (Jeannie, I'll never forget you), Dr. Mickley, Kathryn Frazier, Matt Bauerschmidt, and everyone else.

To Chris and Jennifer Smith: I'm so glad I got you as godparents.

Thank you to Mattie Kahn, who originally saw a story worth sharing.

Thank you to my AP US history teacher, Miss Samuelson, who pulled me aside after class when I was struggling with anorexia at seventeen. Rest in peace.

To my dog, Samson, who was the catalyst for so much healing and so much needed change. Thank you for pulling me out of my self and rooting me in reality. Thank you for loving me endlessly. I wouldn't be here without you. It's not a coincidence that *dog* is *God* spelled backwards.

To Jackie P. for loving me just as I am—what a rare and precious thing. You are my gem.

And, of course . . . thank you to the readers and consumers of my work, from *For the Love of Peanut Butter* to @leefromamerica to now. I wouldn't be here without you. Thank you for watching, sharing, clicking, screenshotting, lurking, liking, commenting, and feeling something when you came across my posts.

Maybe it was parasocial. But it was also real. And that's what makes it so weird and holy.

About the Author

LEE TILGHMAN began blogging when she was seventeen, amassing a large following for her blogs *For the Love of Peanut Butter* and *Lee From America*, both of which helped shape the early wellness influencer landscape. She was born and raised in Connecticut and currently lives in Brooklyn, New York. This is her first book.

1

2

3

4

5

6

7

8

13

14

15

16

17

18

19

20

21

22

23

24

25

26

27

28